I0128846

Charles F. Deems, Phoebe Cary

Hymns for all Christians

Charles F. Deems, Phoebe Cary

Hymns for all Christians

ISBN/EAN: 9783744779340

Printed in Europe, USA, Canada, Australia, Japan

Cover: Foto ©Thomas Meinert / pixelio.de

More available books at **www.hansebooks.com**

HYMNS

FOR

ALL CHRISTIANS.

COMPILED BY

CHARLES F. DEEMS,

AND

PHŒBE CARY.

"Let the people praise Thee, O God; let *all* the people praise Thee."
.... Psalm lxvii. 3. . . . .

THIRD EDITION.

NEW YORK:

PUBLISHED BY HURD AND HOUGHTON.

Cambridge: Riverside Press.

1874.

Entered according to Act of Congress, in the year 1869, by
HURD AND HOUGHTON,
In the Clerk's Office of the District Court for the Southern District of
New York.

RIVERSIDE, CAMBRIDGE:
STEREOTYPED AND PRINTED BY
H. O. HOUGHTON AND COMPANY

PREFACE.

THIS compilation is not intended to supplant any collection now in use, but rather to serve all Christians by putting in their hands a convenient manual, embracing all the best and most used Hymns of all branches of the Church of Christ.

Of other books, it must have been generally noticed that the larger are cumbered with very many hymns, which, because of their meter or their lack of poetical or devotional worth, are never used. The smaller compilations are either sectarian or carelessly made, without regard to the wants of Christians generally, and apparently with no high standard of excellence.

In this book the classification has been made according to the apostolic category of Hymns, and Spiritual Songs, and Psalms. (Col. iii. 16.) It was agreed that each Hymn should be a metrical address to God ; that the Spiritual Songs should have more latitude of signification, embracing whatever might be edifying in social singing; and that among the Psalms should be admitted many such as should more usually be "said" rather than "sung." To the best of the knowledge, judgment, and taste of my gifted co-worker and myself, the one hundred *best* Hymns have been selected according to their poetical excellence, their devotional fervor, and their popularity. Sometimes one of these character-istics has been so manifest as to secure our ver-dict in the absence of the two others; but in no case have we admitted a Hymn which we did not believe to be in accordance with "the mind of the Spirit," as set forth in the Word of God, nor one that might not be sung in all its parts by all the people in the service of the sanctuary. Among the Spiritual Songs have been inserted some which hold their place by their popularity. The compilers did not choose to let their stand-ard pronounce a final judgment against what thousands had found edifying or pleasant; but in no case, it is thought, has this feeling secured the admission of what will seem offensive to pure taste. The best one hundred Spiritual Songs have thus been obtained. The Psalms have been called Lyrics, as the former title has

obtained a specific designation, perhaps somewhat more narrow than the design of this book.
 The aid of many friends in the several branches of Christ's Church is most gratefully acknowledged; but thus generally, because there is not space to designate the obligations which each kind helper has imposed. Finally, nothing was admitted upon which Miss Cary and myself did not agree; and if any special favorite is missed by any reader, let him know that he has the sympathy of each compiler, for each has had some pet thing thrown out by what seemed the obstinate want of taste or judgment in the other: but by this independence of judgment and faithfulness of criticism we believe that we have secured what we confidently hope the Christian world will pronounce, *upon the whole*, the best three hundred devotional poems extant.

The work has been done with conscientious fidelity. At first it was thought quite easy to find what was needed. But the labor grew. Months have been given to reading, comparison, and correspondence; about twenty thousand metrical compositions in English, German, and Latin have been examined; and this book is the result.

PREFACE.

Having yielded to Miss Cary's importunity that this Preface be written in my own name, and contain the statement that much of the labor has fallen upon my hands, I cannot be denied the pleasure of saying that Miss Cary has frequently and carefully reviewed every line of this volume with me, and that to her fine poetic taste the Christian public must feel indebted for much that appears in this book, and perhaps still more for what has been excluded.

CHARLES F. DEEMS.

' CHURCH OF THE STRANGERS,''
.New York, 1869.

HYMNS.

[By CHARLES WESLEY, born 1709; died 1788.]

A CHARGE to keep I have,
    A God to glorify ;
A never-dying soul to save,
    And fit it for the sky.
To serve the present age,
    My calling to fulfill, —
O may it all my powers engage,
    To do my Master's will.

2 Arm me with jealous care,
    As in Thy sight to live ;
And O, thy servant, Lord, prepare,
    A strict account to give.
Help me to watch and pray,
    And on Thyself rely,
Assured, if I my trust betray,
    I shall forever die.

1

2　　　*In Memory of Jesus.*　　　C. M.

By JAMES MONTGOMERY, England, born 1771; died 1854. A paraphrase
of Luke xxii. 19.]

ACCORDING to Thy gracious word,
In meek humility,
This will I do, my dying Lord, —
I will remember Thee.

2 Thy body, broken for my sake,
My bread from heaven shall be :
Thy testamental cup I take,
And thus remember Thee.

3 Remember Thee and all Thy pains,
And all Thy love to me ;
Yea, while a breath, a pulse remains,
Will I remember Thee.

4 And when these failing lips grow dumb,
And mind and mem'ry flee,
When Thou shalt in Thy kingdom come,
Jesus, remember me.

3　　　*Surrender at the Cross.*　　　C. M.

[By ISAAC WATTS, D. D., a Non-conformist English minister, born 1674
died 1726. This hymn was written in 1709.]

ALAS ! and did my Saviour bleed?
And did my Sov'reign die?
Would He devote that sacred head
For such a worm as I ?

2 Was it for crimes that I have done,
He groan'd upon the tree ?

Amazing pity! grace unknown!
   And love beyond degree!

3 Well might the sun in darkness hide,
   And shut his glories in,
When Christ, the mighty Maker, died,
   For man's, the creature's, sin.

4 Thus might I hide my blushing face
   While His dear cross appears,
Dissolve my heart in thankfulness,
   And melt mine eyes to tears.

5 But drops of grief can ne'er repay
   The debt of love I owe:
Here, Lord, I give myself away, —
   'Tis all that I can do.

4   *Morning.*   L. M.

[By Bishop Ken, of England, born 1667, died 1711. Written for the Winchester School. The last stanza has probably been sung more frequently than any other four lines in the language, and is, by some of the best critics, pronounced the finest Doxology in the English tongue.]

ALL praise to Thee, who safe hast kept,
   And hast refreshed me whilst I slept;
Grant, Lord, when I from death shall wake,
I may of endless light partake.

2 Lord, I my vows to Thee renew:
Disperse my sins as morning dew,
Guard my first springs of thought and will,
And with Thyself my spirit fill.

3 Direct, control, suggest this day,
All I design, or do, or say,

That all my powers, with all their might,
In Thy sole glory may unite.

4 Praise God from whom all blessings flow :
Praise Him, all creatures here below :
Praise Him above, ye heavenly host :
Praise Father, Son, and Holy Ghost.

5　　　　　*Evening.*　　　　L. M.

[By BISHOP KEN.]

A LL praise to Thee, my God, this night,
For all the blessings of the light!
Keep me, O keep me, King of kings,
Under Thine own almighty wings.

2 Forgive me, Lord, for Thy dear Son,
The ills that I this day have done —
That with the world, myself, and Thee,
I, ere I sleep, at peace may be.

3 Teach me to live, that I may dread
The grave as little as my bed ;
Teach me to die, that so I may
Rise glorious at the awful day.

4 O may my soul on Thee repose,
And with sweet sleep mine eyelids close —
Sleep, that may me more vigorous make
To serve my God when I awake.

5 Praise God, from whom all blessings flow :
Praise Him, all creatures here below :
Praise Him above, ye heavenly host :
Praise Father, Son, and Holy Ghost!

Yielding to Love. S. M.
[By CHARLES WESLEY.]

AND can I yet delay
My little all to give?
To tear my soul from earth away
For Jesus to receive?

2 Nay, but I yield, I yield;
I can hold out no more:
I sink, by dying love compell'd,
And own Thee conqueror.

3 Though late, I all forsake;
My friends, my all, resign :
Gracious Redeemer, take, O take,
And seal me ever Thine.

4 Come and possess me whole,
Nor hence again remove;
Settle and fix my wav'ring soul
With all Thy weight of love.

5 My one desire be this, —
Thy only love to know;
To seek and taste no other bliss,
No other good below.

6 My life, my portion Thou;
Thou all-sufficient art:
My hope, my heavenly treasure, now
Enter, and keep my heart.

7   *The New Body.*   S. M.

[By Dr. Isaac Watts.]

AND must this body die —
This well-wrought frame decay?
And must these active limbs of mine
Lie mould'ring in the clay?

2 Corruption, earth, and worms,
  Shall but refine this flesh,
Till my triumphant spirit comes
  To put it on afresh.

3 God my Redeemer lives,
  And ever from the skies,
Looks down and watches all my dust,
  Till He shall bid it rise.

4 Array'd in glorious grace
  Shall these vile bodies shine,
And every shape and every face,
  Be heavenly and divine.

5 These lively hopes we owe,
  Lord, to Thy dying love:
O may we bless Thy grace below,
  And sing Thy grace above!

6 Saviour, accept the praise
  Of these our humble songs,
Till tunes of nobler sound we raise
  With our immortal tongues.

8   *Seeing the Invisible.*   **L. M.**

[By CHARLES WESLEY.]

AUTHOR of faith, eternal Word,
  Whose Spirit breathes the active flame,
Faith, — like its finisher and Lord,
To-day, as yesterday, the same : —

2 To Thee our humble hearts aspire,
  And ask the gift unspeakable ;
Increase in us the kindled fire,
  In us the work of faith fulfill.

3 By faith we know Thee strong to save : —
  Save us, a present Saviour Thou ! —
Whate'er we hope, by faith we have ;
  Future, and past, subsisting now.

4 To him that in thy Name believes
  Eternal life with Thee is given ;
Into himself he all receives, —
  Pardon, and holiness, and heaven.

5 The things unknown to feeble sense,
  Unseen by reason's glimm'ring ray,
With strong commanding evidence,
  Their heavenly origin display.

6 Faith lends its realizing light ;
  The clouds disperse, the shadows fly ;
Th' Invisible appears in sight,
  And God is seen by mortal eye.

7

9   *Adoration.*   **L. M.**

[By Dr. WATTS. Let this hymn never be sung to any other tune than " Old Hundred."]

BEFORE Jehovah's awful throne,
     Ye nations bow with sacred joy;
Know that the Lord is God alone,
     He can create, and He destroy.

2 His sovereign power, without our aid,
     Made us of clay, and form'd us men;
And when like wandering sheep we stray'd,
     He brought us to His fold again.

3 We'll crowd Thy gates with thankful songs,
     High as the heavens our voices raise;
And earth, with her ten thousand tongues,
     Shall fill Thy courts with sounding praise.

4 Wide as the world is Thy command;
     Vast as eternity Thy love;
Firm as a rock Thy truth shall stand,
     When rolling years shall cease to move.

10   *The Spirit Enlightens.*   **C. M.**

[By CHARLES WESLEY.]

COME, Holy Ghost, our hearts inspire;
     Let us Thine influence prove; —
Source of the old prophetic fire;
     Fountain of life and love.

2 Come, Holy Ghost, for moved by Thee
     The prophets wrote and spoke:

Unlock the truth, Thyself the key;
Unseal the sacred book.

3 Expand Thy wings, Celestial Dove;
Brood o'er our nature's night;
On our disorder'd spirits move,
And let there now be light.

4 God, through Himself, we then shall know,
If Thou within us shine;
And sound, with all Thy saints below,
The depths of love divine.

11 *The Spirit Quickens.* C. M.
[By Dr. WATTS.]

COME, Holy Spirit, heavenly Dove,
With all Thy quick'ning powers:
Kindle a flame of sacred love
In these cold hearts of ours.

2 Look how we grovel here below,
Fond of these earthly toys;
Our souls, how heavily they go,
To reach eternal joys.

3 In vain we tune our formal songs, —
In vain we strive to rise;
Hosannas languish on our tongues,
And our devotion dies.

4 Father, and shall we ever live
At this poor dying rate;
Our love so faint, so cold to Thee,
And Thine to us so great?

5 Come, Holy Spirit, heavenly Dove,
    With all Thy quick'ning powers ;
Come, shed abroad a Saviour's love,
    And that shall kindle ours.

12   *Renewing the Covenant.*   C. M.
                [By CHARLES WESLEY.]

COME, let us use the grace divine,
    And all, with one accord,
In a perpetual cov'nant join
    Ourselves to Christ the Lord ;

2 Give up ourselves, through Jesus' power,
    His Name to glorify ;
And promise, in this sacred hour,
    For God to live and die.

3 The cov'nant we this moment make
    Be ever kept in mind ;
We will no more our God forsake,
    Or cast His words behind.

4 We never will throw off His fear,
    Who hears our solemn vow ;
And if thou art well pleased to hear,
    Come down, and meet us now.

5 Thee, Father, Son, and Holy Ghost,
    Let all our hearts receive ;
Present with the celestial host,
    The peaceful answer give.

6 To each the cov'nant blood apply,
    Which takes our sins away ;

And register our names on high,
And keep us to that day.

13   *Wrestling Jacob.*   P. M,
[By Charles Wesley.]

COME, O thou Traveler unknown,
   Whom still I hold, but cannot see ;
My company before is gone,
   And I am left alone with Thee:
With Thee all night I mean to stay,
And wrestle till the break of day.

2 I need not tell Thee who I am ;
   My sin and misery declare ;
Thyself hast call'd me by my name ;
   Look on Thy hands, and read it there:
But who, I ask Thee, who art Thou ?
Tell me Thy name, and tell me now.

3 In vain Thou strugglest to be free ;
   I never will unloose my hold !
Art Thou the Man that died for me ?
   The secret of Thy love unfold:
Till I Thy name and nature know,
Wrestling, I will not let Thee go.

4 Yield to me now, for I am weak,
   But confident in self-despair ;
Speak to my heart, in blessings speak,
   Be conquer'd by my instant prayer :
Speak, or Thou never hence shall move,
And tell me if Thy name is Love.

2   11

5 'Tis Love! 'tis Love! Thou diedst for me!
I hear Thy whisper in my heart!
The morning breaks, the shadows flee,
  Pure, universal Love Thou art;
In vain I have not wept nor strove;
Thy nature and Thy name is Love.

14 *Invocation.* P. M.

[The national British song of " God Save the King," appeared first in the " Gentlemen's Magazine " in 1745. About nineteen years afterwards appeared this hymn to the same tune, in a collection by Rev. Spencer Madan, but there is no evidence that he was the author.]

COME, Thou Almighty King,
  Help us Thy Name to sing
  Help us to praise:
Father all glorious,
O'er all victorious,
Come, and reign over us,
  Ancient of days.

2 Jesus, our Lord, arise,
Scatter our enemies,
  And make them fall;
Let Thine almighty aid
Our sure defense be made;
Our souls on Thee be stay'd;
  Lord, hear our call.

3 Come, Thou incarnate Word,
Gird on Thy mighty sword,
  Our prayer attend;
Come, and Thy people bless,

And give Thy word success :
Spirit of holiness,
    On us descend.

4 Come, Holy Comforter,
Thy sacred witness bear
    In this glad hour :
Thou who Almighty art,
Now rule in every heart,
And ne'er from us depart,
    Spirit of power.

5 To the great One and Three
Eternal praises be
    Hence, evermore.
His sovereign majesty
May we in glory see,
And to eternity
    Love and adore.

15   *"Come, Thou Fount."*   P. M.

[By Rev. ROBERT ROBINSON, an eccentric English Independent, once a
follower of Whitefield. This favorite hymn was written in early life. He
afterwards became irreligious. One day, while travelling in a stage-coach,
a lady, not knowing who he was, called his attention to this hymn in a
book she was reading. He endeavored to change the conversation. When
she reverted to the subject, he burst into tears and said, " Madam, I am
the unhappy man that wrote that hymn; and I would give a thousand
worlds to enjoy the feelings I then had."]

COME, Thou Fount of every blessing,
    Tune my heart to sing Thy grace :
Streams of mercy, never ceasing,
    Call for songs of loudest praise.
Teach me some melodious sonnet,
    Sung by flaming tongues above :

Praise the mount — I'm fixed upon it;
Mount of Thy redeeming love!

2 Here I'll raise mine Ebenezer;
    Hither by Thy help I'm come;
And I hope, by Thy good pleasure,
    Safely to arrive at home.
Jesus sought me when a stranger,
    Wand'ring from the fold of God;
He, to rescue me from danger,
    Interposed His precious blood.

3 O! to grace how great a debtor.
    Daily I'm constrained to be!
Let Thy goodness, like a fetter,
    Bind my wand'ring heart to Thee:
Prone to wander, Lord, I feel it —
    Prone to leave the God I love;
Here's my heart, O take and seal it;
    Seal it for Thy courts above.

16   *"Thou knowest that I love Thee."*   **C. M.**

[By Dr. DODDRIDGE. Suggested by John xxi. 15-17.]

DO not I love Thee, O my Lord?
    Behold my heart and see;
And turn the dearest idol out
    That dares to rival Thee.

2 Do not I love Thee from my soul?
    Then let me nothing love:
Dead be my heart to every joy
    When Jesus cannot move.

3 Is not Thy name melodious still
　To mine attentive ear?
Doth not each pulse with pleasure bound
　My Saviour's voice to hear?

4 Hast Thou a lamb in all thy flock
　I would disdain to feed?
Hast Thou a foe before whose face
　I fear Thy cause to plead?

5 Would not my heart pour forth its blood
　In honor of Thy Name?
And challenge the cold hand of death
　To damp th' immortal flame?

6 Thou know'st I love Thee, dearest Lord;
　But O I long to soar
Far from the sphere of mortal joys,
　And learn to love Thee more.

17　　　　　*Solemn Reverence.*　　　L. M.

[By Dr. WATTS.]

ETERNAL Power, whose high abode
　Becomes the grandeur of a God;
Infinite lengths, beyond the bounds
Where stars revolve their little rounds.

2 Thee while the first archangel sings,
He hides his face behind his wings:
And ranks of shining thrones around
Fall worshipping, and spread the ground.

3 Lord, what shall earth and ashes do?
We would adore our Maker too;

From sin and dust to Thee we cry,
The Great, the Holy, and the High.

4 Earth, from afar, hath heard Thy fame,
And worms have learn'd to lisp Thy name:
But O ! the glories of Thy mind
Leave all our soaring thoughts behind.

5 God is in heaven, and men below;
Be short our tunes; our words be few:
A solemn reverence checks our songs,
And praise sits silent on our tongues.

18 *Glory and Grace.* **C. M.**

[By Dr. WATTS.]

FATHER, how wide Thy glory shines,
How high Thy wonders rise!
Known through the earth by thousand signs,
By thousands through the skies.

2 Part of Thy Name divinely stands,
On all Thy creatures writ;
They show the labor of Thy hands,
Or impress of Thy feet:

3 But when we view Thy strange design
To save rebellious worms,
Where vengeance and compassion join
In their divinest forms —

4 Here the whole Deity is known,
Nor dares a creature guess
Which of the glories brighter shone,
The justice or the grace.

5 Now the full glories of the Lamb
   Adorn the heavenly plains ;
Bright seraphs learn Immanuel's name,
   And try their choicest strains.

6 O may I bear some humble part
   In that immortal song!
Wonder and joy shall tune my heart,
   And love command my tongue.

19   *Earnestness.*   C. M.

[By CHARLES WESLEY.]

FATHER, I stretch my hands to Thee :
   No other help I know :
If Thou withdraw Thyself from me,
   Ah! whither shall I go?

2 What did Thine only Son endure,
   Before I drew my breath!
What pain, what labor, to secure
   My soul from endless death!

3 O Jesus, could I this believe,
   I now should feel Thy power ;
Now my poor soul Thou wouldst retrieve,
   Nor let me wait one hour.

4 Author of faith! to Thee I lift
   My weary, longing eyes :
O let me now receive that gift, —
   My soul without it dies.

5 Surely Thou canst not let me die!
   O speak, and I shall live!

And here I will unwearied lie,
Till Thou Thy Spirit give.

6 The worst of sinners would rejoice
Could they but see Thy face;
Now let me hear Thy quick'ning voice,
And taste Thy pard'ning grace.

20　　　*The Holy Scriptures.*　　C. M

[By Miss ANNE STEELE, of England, born 1717.]

FATHER of mercies, in Thy word
What endless glory shines;
Forever be Thy Name adored
For these celestial lines.

2 Here may the wretched sons of want
Exhaustless riches find;
Riches above what earth can grant,
And lasting as the mind.

3 Here the fair tree of knowledge grows,
And yields a free repast;
Sublimer sweets than nature knows
Invite the longing taste.

4 Here the Redeemer's welcome voice
Spreads heavenly peace around;
And life, and everlasting joys
Attend the blissful sound.

5 O may these heavenly pages be
Our ever dear delight;
And still new beauties may we see,
And still increasing light.

6 Divine Instructor, gracious Lord,
  Be Thou forever near ;
Teach us to love Thy sacred word,
And view the Saviour there.

21   *Submission.*   C. M.
        [By Miss ANNE STEELE.]

FATHER, whate'er of earthly bliss
    Thy sovereign will denies,
Accepted at Thy throne of grace,
Let this petition rise : —

2 Give me a calm, a thankful heart,
  From every murmur free :
The blessings of Thy grace impart,
And make me live to Thee.

3 Let the sweet hope that Thou art mine
  My life and death attend :
Thy presence through my journey shine,
And crown my journey's end.

22   *Universal Praise.*   L. M.
           [By Dr. WATTS.]

FROM all that dwell below the skies
    Let the Creator's praise arise ;
Let the Redeemer's name be sung
Through every land, by every tongue.

2 Eternal are Thy mercies, Lord ;
  Eternal truth attends Thy word :
Thy praise shall sound from shore to shore,
Till suns shall rise and set no more.

3 Your lofty themes, ye mortals, bring;
  In songs of praise divinely sing;
  The great salvation loud proclaim,
  And shout for joy the Saviour's name.

4 In every land begin the song;
  To every land the strains belong:
  In cheerful sounds all voices raise,
  And fill the world with loudest praise.

23   *Waters of Salvation.*   C. M.

[By CHARLES WESLEY.]

FOUNTAIN of life, to all below
  Let Thy salvation roll;
Water, replenish, and o'erflow
  Every believing soul.

2 Into that happy number, Lord,
  Us weary sinners take;
Jesus, fulfill Thy gracious word,
  For Thine own mercy's sake.

3 The well of life to us Thou art, —
  Of joy, the swelling flood;
Wafted by Thee, with willing heart,
  We swift return to God.

4 We soon shall reach the boundless sea;
  Into Thy fullness fall;
Be lost and swallowed up in Thee, —
  Our God, our All in All.

24   *Child's Hymn.*   7s.

[By CHARLES WESLEY.]

G ENTLE Jesus, meek and mild,
   Look upon a little child ;
Pity my simplicity,
Suffer me to come to Thee.

2 Hide me, from all evil hide,
Self, and stubbornness, and pride ;
Let me live without offense ;
Guard my helpless innocence.

3 Loving Jesus, gentle Lamb,
In Thy gracious hands I am ;
Make me, Saviour, what Thou art ;
Live Thyself within my heart.

4 I shall then show forth Thy praise ;
Serve Thee all my happy days ;
Then the world shall always see
Christ the holy Child in me.

25   *Without God.*   C. M.

[By CHARLES WESLEY.]

G OD is in this and every place ;
   But O, how dark and void
To me ! — 'tis one great wilderness,
This earth without my God.

2 Empty of Him who all things fills,
Till He His light impart,—
Till He His glorious self reveals, —
The veil is on my heart.

3 O Thou who seest and know'st my grief,
   Thyself unseen, unknown,
Pity my helpless unbelief,
   And break my heart of stone.

4 Regard me with a gracious eye;
   The long-sought blessing give;
And bid me, at the point to die,
   Behold Thy face and live.

26   *God of my Life.*   **L. M.**

[BY CHARLES WESLEY.]

GOD of my life, whose gracious power
   Through varied deaths my soul hath led,
Or turn'd aside the fatal hour,
   Or lifted up my sinking head;

2 In all my ways Thy hand I own;
   Thy ruling providence I see;
Assist me still my course to run,
   And still direct my paths to Thee.

3 Whither, O whither should I fly,
   But to my loving Saviour's breast!
Secure within Thine arms to lie,
   And safe beneath Thy wings to rest.

4 I have no skill the snare to shun,
   But Thou, O Christ, my wisdom art:
I ever into ruin run,
   But Thou art greater than my heart

5 Foolish, and impotent, and blind,
   Lead me a way I have not known;

Bring me where I my heaven may find, —
The heaven of loving Thee alone.

27   *" Holy Father."*   L. M.
[By Dr. WATTS.]

GREAT God, indulge my humble claim;
   Be Thou my hope, my joy, my rest;
The glories that compose Thy name
   Stand all engaged to make me blest.

2 Thou great and good, Thou just and wise,
   Thou art my Father and my God;
And I am Thine by sacred ties,
   Thy son, Thy servant bought with blood.

3 With heart and eyes, and lifted hands,
   For Thee I long, to Thee I look;
As travellers in thirsty lands
   Pant for the cooling water-brook.

4 I'll lift my hands, I'll raise my voice,
   While I have breath to pray or praise;
This work shall make my heart rejoice,
   And fill the remnant of my days.

28   *" The Living God."*   C. M.
[By Dr. WATTS.]

GREAT God! how infinite art Thou!
   What worthless mortals we!
Let the whole race of creatures bow,
   And pay their praise to Thee.

2. Thy throne eternal ages stood,
   Ere seas or stars were made;

23

Thou art the ever-living God,
   Were all the nations dead.

3 Eternity, with all its years,
   Stands present in Thy view;
To Thee there's nothing old appears,
   Great God! there's nothing new.

4 Our lives through various scenes are drawn,
   And vexed with trifling cares;
While Thine eternal thoughts move on
   Thine undisturbed affairs.

5 Great God! how infinite art Thou!
   What worthless mortals we!
Let the whole race of creatures bow,
   And pay their praise to Thee.

29   *Delight in Worship.*   · **L. M.**

[By Dr. WATTS. Paraphrase of Psalm 84.]

GREAT God, attend, while Zion sings
   The joy that from Thy presence springs;
To spend one day with Thee on earth
Exceeds a thousand days of mirth.

2 Might I enjoy the meanest place
Within Thy house, O God of grace,
Not tents of ease, or thrones of power,
Should tempt my feet to leave Thy door.

3 God is our sun, He makes our day;
God is our shield, He guards our way
From all assaults of hell and sin,
From foes without and foes within.

24

4 All needful grace will God bestow,
And crown that grace with glory too ;
He gives us all things, and withholds
No real good from upright souls.

5 O God our King, whose sovereign sway
The glorious hosts of heaven obey,
And devils at Thy presence flee,
Blest is the man that trusts in Thee.

30 *Guide Me.* P. M.
[By Rev. WILLIAM WILLIAMS, of Wales, born 1717; died 1791.]

GUIDE me, O Thou great Jehovah,
 Pilgrim through this barren land :
I am weak — but Thou art mighty,
 Hold me with Thy powerful hand :
 Bread of heaven,
 Feed me till I want no more.

2 Open now the crystal fountain,
 Whence the healing waters flow ;
Let the fiery, cloudy pillar,
 Lead me all my journey through :
 Strong Deliv'rer,
 Be Thou still my strength and shield.

3 When I tread the verge of Jordan,
 Bid my anxious fears subside :
Bear me through the swelling current ;
 Land me safe on Canaan's side :
 Songs of praises
 I will ever give to Thee.

31　　　　　　*Help my Unbelief.*　　　　C. M.

[By Dr. Watts.]

HOW sweet a voice of sov'reign grace
　　Sounds from the sacred word! —
Ho! ye despairing sinners, come,
　　And trust a faithful Lord.

2 My soul obeys the gracious call,
　　And runs to this relief;
I would believe Thy promise, Lord;
　　O help my unbelief!

3 To the blest fountain of Thy blood,
　　Incarnate God, I fly;
Here let me wash my guilty soul
　　From crimes of deepest dye.

4 A guilty, weak, and helpless worm,
　　Into Thine arms I fall;
Be Thou my strength and righteousness,
　　My Jesus, and my all.

32　　　　　　*The Precious Name.*　　　　C. M.

[By Rev. John Newton, born 1725; died 1807. The friend and pastor of Cowper, who with Newton wrote the celebrated " Olney Hymns."

HOW sweet the name of Jesus sounds
　　In a believer's ear!
It soothes his sorrows, heals his wounds,
　　And drives away his fear.

2 It makes the wounded spirit whole,
　　And calms the troubled breast;

'Tis manna to the hungry soul,
And to the weary, rest.

3 Dear Name, the rock on which I build,
My shield and hiding-place ;
My never-failing treasure, fill'd
With boundless stores of grace :

4 Weak is the effort of my heart,
And cold my warmest thought;
But when I see Thee as Thou art,
I'll praise Thee as I ought.

5 Till then I would Thy love proclaim
With every fleeting breath;
And may the music of Thy name
Refresh my soul in death.

33 *Love for the Church.* **S. M.**

[By Rev. TIMOTHY DWIGHT, D. D., born in Massachusetts, 1752 ;
died, 1817. Paraphrase of Psalm 137.]

I LOVE Thy kingdom, Lord,
The house of Thine abode,
The church our blest Redeemer saved
With His own precious blood.

2 I love Thy Church, O God!
Her walls before Thee stand
Dear as the apple of Thine eye,
And graven on Thy hand.

3 For her my tears shall fall ;
For her my prayers ascend ;
To her my cares and toils be given
Till toils and cares shall end.

4 Beyond my highest joy
  I prize her heavenly ways;
Her sweet communion, solemn vows,
  Her hymns of love and praise.

5 Sure as Thy truth shall last,
  To Zion shall be given
The brightest glories earth can yield,
  And brighter bliss of heaven.

34 *For a tender Conscience.* C. M.

[BY CHARLES WESLEY.]

I WANT a principle within
  Of jealous, godly fear,
A sensibility of sin,
  A pain to feel it near.

2 I want the first approach to feel
  Of pride or fond desire, —
To catch the wand'ring of my will,
  And quench the kindling fire.

3 From Thee that I no more may part,
  No more Thy goodness grieve,
The filial awe, the fleshly heart,
  The tender conscience give.

4 Quick as the apple of an eye,
  O God, my conscience make!
Awake my soul when sin is nigh,
  And keep it still awake.

5 If to the right or left I stray,
  That moment, Lord, reprove,

And let me weep my life away
For having grieved Thy love.

6 O may the least omission pain
My well-instructed soul;
And drive me to the blood again
Which makes the wounded whole!

35 *Ashamed of Jesus.* **L. M.**

[By Rev. JOSEPH GRIGG, of England; died 1768.]

JESUS, and shall it ever be,
A mortal man ashamed of Thee!
Ashamed of Thee, whom angels praise, —
Whose glories shine through endless days?

2 Ashamed of Jesus! sooner far
Let evening blush to own a star:
He sheds the beams of light divine
O'er this benighted soul of mine.

3 Ashamed of Jesus! just as soon
Let midnight be ashamed of noon:
'Tis midnight with my soul till He,
Bright Morning Star, bid darkness flee.

4 Ashamed of Jesus! — that dear Friend
On whom my hopes of heaven depend;
No! — when I blush be this my shame
That I no more revere His Name.

5 Ashamed of Jesus! — yes, I may,
When I've no guilt to wash away;
No tear to wipe, no good to crave,
No fears to quell, no soul to save.

6 Till then — nor is my boasting vain —
Till then, I boast a Saviour slain;
And O, may this my glory be, —
That Christ is not ashamed of me.

36 *The Charming Name.* **C. M.**

[By PHILIP DODDRIDGE, D. D., a Dissenting minister of England;
born 1702; died 1751.]

JESUS, I love Thy charming name,
'Tis music to my ear:
Fain would I sound it out so loud
That earth and heaven should hear.

2 Yes, Thou art precious to my soul,
My transport and my trust:
Jewels, to Thee, are gaudy toys,
And gold is sordid dust.

3 All my capacious powers can wish
In Thee doth richly meet;
Nor to mine eyes is light so dear,
Nor friendship half so sweet.

4 Thy grace still dwells upon my heart,
And sheds its fragrance there:
The noblest balm of all its wounds,
The cordial of its care.

5 I'll speak the honors of Thy Name
With my last laboring breath:
Then speechless clasp Thee in mine arms,
The antidote of death.

37   *Contrition.*   **P. M.**

[By CHARLES WESLEY.]

JESUS, let Thy pitying eye
    Call back a wand'ring sheep;
False to Thee, like Peter, I
    Would fain like Peter weep.
Let me be by grace restored:
    On me be all long-suff'ring shown;
Turn, and look upon me, Lord,
    And break my heart of stone.

2 Saviour, Prince, enthroned above,
    Repentance to impart,
Give me, through Thy dying love,
    The humble, contrite heart:
Give what I have long implored,
    A portion of Thy grief unknown:
Turn, and look upon me, Lord,
    And break my heart of stone.

3 For Thine own compassion's sake,
    The gracious wonder show;
Cast my sins behind Thy back,
    And wash me white as snow;
If Thy bowels now are stirr'd,
    If now I do myself bemoan,
Turn, and look upon me, Lord,
    And break my heart of stone.

38   *The only Refuge.*   **P. M.**

[By CHARLES WESLEY.]

JESUS, Lover of my soul,
    Let me to Thy bosom fly,

While the nearer waters roll,
    While the tempest still is high;
Hide me, O my Saviour, hide,
    Till the storm of life be past;
Safe into the haven guide,
    O receive my soul at last.

2 Other refuge have I none;
    Hangs my helpless soul on Thee:
Leave, O leave me not alone;
    Still support and comfort me:
All my trust on Thee is stay'd;
    All my help from Thee I bring;
Cover my defenseless head
    With the shadow of Thy wing.

3 Thou, O Christ, art all I want:
    More than all in Thee I find:
Raise the fallen, cheer the faint,
    Heal the sick, and lead the blind.
Just and holy is Thy name;
    I am all unrighteousness;
False and full of sin I am;
    Thou art full of truth and grace.

4 Plenteous grace with Thee is found, —
    Grace to cover all my sin:
Let the healing streams abound;
    Make and keep me pure within.
Thou of life the fountain art;
    Freely let me take of Thee:
Spring Thou up within my heart;
    Rise to all eternity.

39 *The Truth and Way.* S. M.

[By CHARLES WESLEY.]

JESUS, my truth, my way,
My sure, unerring light,
On Thee my feeble steps I stay,
Which Thou wilt guide aright.

2 My wisdom and my guide,
My counselor Thou art;
O never let me leave Thy side,
Or from Thy paths depart.

3 I lift mine eyes to Thee,
Thou gracious, bleeding Lamb,
That I may now enlighten'd be,
And never put to shame.

4 Never will I remove
Out of Thy hands my cause;
But rest in Thy redeeming love,
And hang upon Thy cross.

5 O make me all like Thee,
Before I hence remove;
Settle, confirm, establish me,
And build me up in love.

6 Let me Thy witness live,
When sin is all destroyed;
And then my spotless soul receive,
And take me home to God.

40 *The Shepherd.* 7s.

JESUS, Shepherd of Thy sheep,
In Thine arms my spirit keep;

I am weak and I am lone:
Jesus, take me for Thine own.

2 In Thy bosom Thou dost bear
Those who most do need Thy **care**;
I the humblest lamb would be, —
I would trust myself to Thee.

3 Fair and lovely to behold
Is Thy lower earthly fold;
Guardian care shall never **fail**
To the flock within its pale.

4 Still my ardent hopes aspire
To that better home and higher
Where from every fold Thy sheep
Thou shalt safely bring and keep.

41   *The Great Name.*   **C. M.**

[By CHARLES WESLEY.]

JESUS, the Name high over all,
In hell, or earth, or sky;
Angels and men before it fall,
And devils fear and fly.

2 Jesus, the Name to sinners dear, —
The Name to sinners given;
It scatters all their guilty fear;
It turns their hell to heaven.

3 Jesus the pris'ner's fetters breaks,
And bruises Satan's head;
Power into strengthless souls he speaks,
And life into the dead.

4 O that the world might taste and see
  The riches of His grace ;
The arms of love that compass me,
  Would all mankind embrace.

5 His only righteousness I show, —
  His saving truth proclaim :
'Tis all my business here below
  To cry, — Behold the Lamb!

6 Happy, if with my latest breath
  I may but gasp his name ;
Preach Him to all, and cry in death,
  Behold, behold the Lamb!

42 *The Sweet Memory.* C. M.

[By St. BERNARD of Clairvaux, who died in 1153. He was called "the Mel-
lifluous Doctor." The original of his hymn begins "Jesu Dulcis Me-
moria," and contains about two hundred lines. It has inspired several of
our modern hymns. This version is by E. Caswall.]

JESUS, the very thought of Thee
  With sweetness fills my breast;
But sweeter far Thy face to see,
  And in Thy presence rest.

2 Nor voice can sing, nor heart can frame,
  Nor can the memory find
A sweeter sound than Thy blest name,
  O Saviour of mankind!

3 O hope of every contrite heart,
  O joy of all the meek,
To those who fall, how kind Thou art!
  How good to those who seek !

4 But what to those who find? ah! this
  Nor tongue nor pen can show :

The love of Jesus, what it is,
None but His loved ones know.

5 Jesus, our only joy be Thou,
As Thou our prize will be ;
Jesus ! be Thou our glory now,
And through eternity.

43   *Unseen, but Loved.*   C. M.

[By RAY PALMER, D. D., born in Rhode Island, 1808. This hymn para-
phrases 1 Pet. i. 8.]

JESUS, these eyes have never seen
That radiant form of Thine !
The veil of sense hangs dark between
Thy blessed face and mine.

2 Like some bright dream that comes unsought,
When slumbers o'er me roll,
Thine image ever fills my thought,
And charms my ravish'd soul.

3 Yet, though I have not seen, and still
Must rest in faith alone,
I love Thee, dearest Lord ! and will,
Unseen, but not Unknown.

4 When death these mortal eyes shall seal,
And still this throbbing heart,
The rending veil shall Thee reveal,
All glorious as Thou art.

44   *Refining Fire.*   C. M.

[By CHARLES WESLEY.]

JESUS, Thine all-victorious love
Shed in my heart abroad :

Then shall my feet no longer rove,
Rooted and fix'd in God.

2 O that in me the sacred fire
Might now begin to glow;
Burn up the dross of base desire,
And make the mountains flow.

3 O that it now from heaven might fall,
And all my sins consume :
Come, Holy Ghost, for Thee I call;
Spirit of burning, come.

4 Refining fire, go through my heart;
Illuminate my soul ;
Scatter Thy life through every part,
And sanctify the whole.

5 My steadfast soul, from falling free,
Shall then no longer move ;
While Christ is all the world to me,
And all my heart is love.

· 45 *Tribute of Praise.* L. M.

[By Dr. WATTS.]

JESUS, Thou everlasting King,
Accept the tribute which we bring;
Accept Thy well-deserved renown,
And wear our praises as Thy crown.

2 Let every act of worship be
Like our espousals, Lord, to Thee ;
Like the blest hour, when from above
We first received the pledge of love.

3 The gladness of that happy day,
O may it ever, ever stay:
Nor let our faith forsake its hold,
Nor hope decline, nor love grow cold.

4 Let every moment, as it flies,
Increase Thy praise, improve our joys,
Till we be raised to sing thy Name,
At the great supper of the Lamb.

46 *Zinzendorf's Hymn.* L. M.

[By Count ZINZENDORF, 1739. This version is by John Wesley. The first
stanza belongs to a German hymn of earlier times than Zinzendorf's, and
is often quoted at the death-bed of Christians in Germany. One word has
been altered.]

JESUS, Thy love and righteousness
My beauty are, my glorious dress:
'Midst flaming worlds, in these array'd,
With joy shall I lift up my head.

2 Bold shall I stand in Thy great day,
For who aught to my charge shall lay?
Fully absolved through these I am, —
From sin and fear, from guilt and shame.

3 The holy, meek, unspotted Lamb,
Who from the Father's bosom came —
Who died for me, e'en me, to atone, —
Now for my Lord and God I own.

4 Lord, I believe Thy precious blood, —
Which, at the mercy-seat of God
Forever doth for sinners plead, —
For me, e'en for my soul, was shed.

5 Lord, I believe were sinners more
Than sands upon the ocean shore,

Thou hast for all a ransom paid,
For all a full atonement made.

47 *The Loadstone of Love.* C, M,
[By CHARLES WESLEY.]

JESUS, united by Thy grace,
And each to each endear'd,
With confidence we seek Thy face,
And know our prayer is heard.

2 Still let us own our common Lord,
And bear Thine easy yoke, —
A band of love, a threefold cord,
Which never can be broke.

3 Touch'd by the loadstone of Thy love,
Let all our hearts agree ;
And ever toward each other move,
And ever move toward Thee.

4 To Thee, inseparably joined,
Let all our spirits cleave ;
O may we all the loving mind
That was in Thee receive.

48 *Claiming the Promise.* S, M.
[By CHARLES WESLEY.]

JESUS, we look to Thee,
Thy promised presence claim :
Thou in the midst of us shalt be,
Assembled in Thy name :

2 Not in the name of pride
Or selfishness we meet ;

From nature's paths we turn aside,
And worldly thoughts forget.

3 We meet the grace to take
Which Thou hast freely given;
We meet on earth for Thy dear sake,
That we may meet in heaven.

4 Present we know Thou art,
But O, thyself reveal!
Now, Lord, let every bounding heart
The mighty comfort feel.

49 *Just as I am.* L. M.

[By Miss CHARLOTTE ELLIOT, of England.]

JUST as I am — without one plea,
But that Thy blood was shed for me,
And that Thou bid'st me come to Thee,
O Lamb of God, I come.

2 Just as I am; and waiting not
To rid my soul of one dark blot —
To Thee, whose blood can cleanse each spot
O Lamb of God, I come.

3 Just as I am, though tossed about
With many a conflict, many a doubt,
With fears within, and foes without —
O Lamb of God, I come.

4 Just as I am — poor, wretched, blind:
Sight, riches, healing of the mind,
Yea, all I need, in *Thee* to find,
O Lamb of God, I come.

5 Just as I am, Thou wilt receive,
Wilt welcome, pardon, cleanse, relieve:
Because Thy promise I believe
     O Lamb of God, I come.

6 Just as I am — Thy love unknown,
Has broken every barrier down:
Now to be Thine, yea, *Thine alone,*
     O Lamb of God, I come.

50   *Just as thou art.*   L. M.

JUST as thou art — without one trace
  Of love, or joy, or inward grace,
Or meetness for that heavenly place,
  O guilty sinner, come, O come!

2 Thy sins I bore on Calvary's tree;
The stripes thy due were laid on me,
That peace and pardon might be free, —
  O wretched sinner, come, O come!

3 Come, leave thy burden at the cross;
Count all thy gains but empty dross:
My grace repays all earthly loss, —
  O needy sinner, come, O come!

4 " The Spirit and the Bride say, Come; "
 Rejoicing saints reëcho, Come!
Who faints, who thirsts, who will, may come;
  Thy Saviour bids thee come, O come!

51   *His Goodness.*   C. M.

[By Dr. WATTS.]

LET every tongue Thy goodness speak,
  Thou sov'reign Lord of all;

Thy strength'ning hands uphold the weak,
  And raise the poor that fall.

2 When sorrows bow the spirit down,
  When virtue lies distress'd   .
Beneath the proud oppressor's frown,
  Thou giv'st the mourner rest.

3 Thou know'st the pains Thy servants feel,
  Thou hear'st Thy children's cry;
And their best wishes to fulfill,
  Thy grace is ever nigh.

4 Thy mercy never shall remove
  From men of heart sincere:
Thou sav'st the souls whose humble love
  Is join'd with holy fear.

5 My lips shall dwell upon Thy praise,
  And spread Thy fame abroad;
Let all the sons of Adam raise
  The honors of their God.

52   *Omniscience.*   **C. M.**

[By Dr. WATTS. Paraphrase of Psalm 139.]

LORD, all I am is known to Thee;
  In vain my soul would try
To shun Thy presence, or to flee
  The notice of Thine eye.

2 Thy all-surrounding sight surveys
  My rising and my rest,
My public walks, my private ways,
  The secrets of my breast.

3 My thoughts lie open to Thee, Lord,
Before they're formed within,
And ere my lips pronounce the word,
Thou know'st the sense I mean.

4 O wondrous knowledge! deep and high:
Where can a creature hide?
Within Thy circling arms I lie,
Beset on every side.

5 So let Thy grace surround me still,
And like a bulwark prove,
To guard my soul from every ill,
Secured by sov'reign love.

53   *Lord, dismiss us.*   P. M.

'By Rev. GEORGE BURDER, of England, born in London in 1752 ; died in
1832 ; one of the founders of the Religious Tract Society.]

L ORD, dismiss us with Thy blessing;
Fill our hearts with joy and peace ;
Let us each, Thy love possessing,
Triumph in redeeming grace ;
O refresh us,
Travelling through this wilderness.

2 Thanks we give, and adoration,
For thy gospel's joyful sound;
May the fruits of Thy salvation
In our hearts and lives abound;
May Thy presence
With us evermore be found.

3 So, whene'er the signal's given
Us from earth to call away,

4   43

Borne on angels' wings to heaven,
Glad the summons to obey,
May we ever
Reign with Christ in endless day.

54   *Pentecost.*   **S. M.**

[By JAMES MONTGOMERY.]

L ORD God, the Holy Ghost!
In this accepted hour,
As on the day of Pentecost,
Descend in all Thy power.

2 We meet with one accord
In our appointed place,
And wait the promise of our Lord,
The Spirit of all grace.

3 Like mighty rushing wind
Upon the waves beneath,
Move with one impulse every mind;
One soul, one feeling breathe.

4 The young. the old, inspire
With wisdom from above;
And give us hearts and tongues of fire,
To pray, and praise, and love.

5 Spirit of light, explore
And chase our gloom away,
With lustre shining more and more
Unto the perfect day.

6 Spirit of truth, be Thou.
In life and death, our guide:
O Spirit of adoption! now
May we be sanctified.

55 *Sunday Morning.* C. M.

[By Dr. WATTS.]

L ORD, in the morning Thou shalt hear
My voice ascending high:
To Thee will I direct my prayer,
To Thee lift up mine eye: —

2 Up to the hills where Christ is gone,
To plead for all His saints;
Presenting, at the Father's throne,
Our songs and our complaints.

3 Now to Thy house will I resort,
To taste Thy mercies there;
I will frequent Thy holy court,
And worship in Thy fear.

4 O may Thy Spirit guide my feet
In ways of righteousness;
Make every path of duty straight,
And plain before my face.

56 *Unclean.* L. M.

[By Dr. WATTS.]

L ORD, we are vile, conceived in sin,
And born unholy and unclean;
Sprung from the man whose guilty fall
Corrupts his race, and taints us all.

2 Behold, we fall before Thy face;
Our only refuge is Thy grace:
No outward forms can make us clean;
The leprosy lies deep within.

3 Nor bleeding bird, nor bleeding beast,
  Nor hyssop branch, nor sprinkling priest,
  Nor running brook, nor flood, nor sea,
  Can wash the dismal stain away.

4 Jesus, Thy blood, Thy blood alone,
  Hath power sufficient to atone ;
  Thy blood can make us white as snow ;
  No Jewish types could cleanse us so.

5 While guilt disturbs and breaks our peace,
  Nor flesh nor soul hath rest or ease ;
  Lord, let us hear Thy pard'ning voice,
  And make these broken hearts rejoice.

57   *Invoking Blessings.*   **P. M.**

[By Rev. WILLIAM HAMMOND, an English Moravian, who died in · ·ŀ]

L ORD, we come before Thee now,
    At Thy feet we humbly bow ;
O, do not our suit disdain :
Shall we seek thee, Lord, in vain ?

2 Lord, on Thee our souls depend ;
  In compassion now descend ;
  Fill our hearts with Thy rich grace,
  Tune our lips to sing Thy praise.

3 Send some message from Thy word
  That may joy and peace afford ;
  Let Thy Spirit now impart
  Full salvation to each heart.

4 Comfort those who weep and mourn ;
  Let the time of joy return :

Those that are cast down lift up ;
Make them strong in faith and hope.

5 Grant that all may seek and find
Thee, a gracious God and kind :
Heal the sick, the captive free ;
Let us all rejoice in Thee.

58   *Our Example.*   L, M,
[By Dr. WATTS.]

MY dear Redeemer, and my Lord,
  I read my duty in Thy Word ;
But in Thy life the law appears,
Drawn out in living characters.

2 Such was Thy truth, and such Thy zeal,
  Such def'rence to Thy Father's will,
Such love, and meekness so divine !
I would transcribe and make them mine.

3 Cold mountains and the midnight air
Witnessed the fervor of Thy prayer :
The desert Thy temptations knew,
Thy conflict, and Thy victory too.

4 Be Thou my pattern ; make me bear
More of Thy gracious image here :
Then God, the Judge, shall own my name
Among the followers of the Lamb.

59   *"Looking unto Jesus."*   P, M,
[By RAY PALMER, D. D.]

MY faith looks up to Thee,
  Thou Lamb of Calvary,
Saviour divine :

Now hear me while I pray,
Take all my guilt away,
O let me from this day
   Be wholly Thine.

2 May Thy rich grace impart
Strength to my fainting heart;
   My zeal inspire:
As Thou hast died for me,
O may my love to Thee
Pure, warm, and changeless be,
   A living fire.

3 While life's dark maze I tread,
And griefs around me spread,
   Be Thou my guide:
Bid darkness turn to day,
Wipe sorrow's tears away,
Nor let me ever stray
   From Thee aside.

60   *Perpetual Blessings.*   **L. M.**
[By Dr. WATTS.]

MY God, how endless is Thy love!
   Thy gifts are every evening new;
And morning mercies from above
   Gently descend like early dew.

2 Thou spread'st the curtains of the night,
   Great Guardian of my sleeping hours;
Thy sov'reign word restores the light,
   And quickens all my drowsy powers.

3. I yield myself to Thy command;
   To Thee devote my nights and days;

Perpetual blessings from Thy hand
Demand perpetual songs of praise.

61   *Steadfast Faith.*   C. M.
[By CHARLES WESLEY.]

MY God, I know, I feel Thee mine,
    And will not quit my claim,
Till all I have is lost in Thine,
    And all renew'd I am.

2 I hold Thee with a trembling hand,
    And will not let Thee go,
'Till steadfastly by faith I stand,
    And all Thy goodness know.

62   *Heaven upon Earth.*   S. M.
[By Dr. WATTS.]

MY God, my life, my love,
    To Thee, to Thee I call:
I cannot live if Thou remove,
    For Thou art all in all.

2 The smilings of Thy face,
    How amiable they are!
'Tis heaven to rest in Thine embrace,
    And nowhere else but there.

3 To Thee, and Thee alone,
    The angels owe their bliss;
They sit around Thy gracious throne,
    And dwell where Jesus is.

4 Not all the harps above
    Can make a heavenly place,

If God His residence remove,
Or but conceal His face.

5 Nor earth, nor all the sky,
Can one delight afford,
Nor yield one drop of real joy,
Without Thy presence, Lord.

6 Thou art the sea of love,
Where all my pleasures roll:
The circle where my passions move,
And centre of my soul.

63   *The All-sufficient Portion.*   C. M.
[By Dr. WATTS.]

MY God, my portion, and my love,
My everlasting All,
I've none but Thee in heaven above,
Or on this earthly ball.

2 What empty things are all the skies,
And this inferior clod!
There's nothing here deserves my joys,
There's nothing like my God.

3 To Thee I owe my wealth, and friends,
And health, and safe abode :
Thanks to Thy Name for meaner things ;
But they are not my God.

4 How vain a toy is glitt'ring wealth,
If once compared with Thee ;
Or what's my safety, or my health,
Or all my friends to me ?

5 Were I possessor of the earth,
  And call'd the stars my own,
Without Thy graces and Thyself,
  I were a wretch undone.

6 Let others stretch their arms like seas,
  And grasp in all the shore;
Grant me the visits of Thy grace,
  And I desire no more.

64   *Triumphant Joy.*   C. M.
              [By Dr. WATTS.]

MY God, the spring of all my joys,
    The life of my delights,
The glory of my brightest days,
  And comfort of my nights:

2 In darkest shades if Thou appear,
  My dawning is begun;
Thou art my soul's bright morning star,
  And Thou my rising sun.

3 The opening heavens around me shine
  With beams of sacred bliss,
If Jesus shows His mercy mine,
  And whispers I am His.

4 My soul would leave this heavy clay
  At that transporting word,
Run up with joy the shining way,
  To see and praise my Lord.

5 Fearless of hell and ghastly death,
  I'd break through every foe;

The wings of love and arms of faith
Would bear me conqu'ror through.

65   ·   *Sustain Me.*   **L. M.**

MY hope, my all, my Saviour Thou;
 To Thee, lo, now my soul I bow;
I feel the bliss Thy wounds impart, —
I find Thee, Saviour, in my heart.

2 Be Thou my strength, — be Thou my way;
Protect me through my life's short day:
In all my acts may wisdom guide,
And keep me, Saviour, near Thy side.

3 In fierce temptation's darkest hour,
Save me from sin and Satan's power;
Tear every idol from Thy throne,
And reign, my Saviour, reign alone.

4 My suff'ring time shall soon be o'er;
Then shall I sigh and weep no more:
My ransom'd soul shall soar away,
To sing Thy praise in endless day.

66   *Praise delightful.*   **C. M.**
[By Dr. WATTS.]

MY Saviour, my almighty Friend,
 When I begin Thy praise,
Where will the growing numbers end, —
The numbers of Thy grace?

2 I trust in Thy eternal word;
Thy goodness I adore:

Send down Thy grace, O blessed Lord,
That I may love Thee more.

3 My feet shall travel all the length
Of the celestial road;
And march with courage, in Thy strength,
To see the Lord my God.

4 Awake! awake! my tuneful powers,
With this delightful song;
And entertain the darkest hours,
Nor think the season long.

67   *"Nearer to Thee."*   P. M.

[By SARAH FLOWER ADAMS, who died in 1848.]

NEARER, my God, to Thee,
  Nearer to Thee:
Ev'n though it be a cross
  That raiseth me,
Still all my song shall be,
Nearer, my God, to Thee,
  Nearer to Thee.

2 Though like a wanderer,
  Daylight all gone,
Darkness be over me,
  My rest a stone,
Yet in my dreams I'd be,
Nearer, my God, to Thee,
  Nearer to Thee.

3 There let the way appear
  Steps up to heaven;

All that Thou sendest me
In mercy given,
Angels to beckon me
Nearer, my God, to Thee,
Nearer to Thee.

4 Then with my waking thoughts,
Bright with Thy praise,
Out of my stony griefs,
Bethel I'll raise ;
So by my woes to be
Nearer, my God, to Thee,
Nearer to Thee.

5 Or if on joyful wing,
Cleaving the sky,
Sun, moon, and stars forgot,
Upward I fly,
Still all my song shall be,
Nearer, my God, to Thee,
Nearer to Thee.

68   *A Parting Blessing.*   **C. M.**

By Rev. THOMAS GIBBONS, D. D., an English Congregationalist: died 1785.]

NOW may the God of peace and love,
Who from th' impris'ning grave
Restored the Shepherd of the sheep,
Omnipotent to save ; —

2 Through the rich merits of that blood
Which He on Calvary spilt,
To make th' eternal cov'nant sure,
On which our hopes are built ; —

3 Perfect our souls in every grace,
  T' accomplish all His will ;
And all that's pleasing in His right
  Inspire us to fulfill.

4 For the great Mediator's sake
  We every blessing pray ;
With glory let His name be crown'd,
  Through heaven's eternal day.

69   *The Spirit Absent.*   **C. M.**

[By WILLIAM COWPER, of England, born 1731 ; died in 1800. He was much
of his life under the cloud of insanity. He wrote the fo.v ring hymn ex-
pressive of his spiritual darkness in one of his lucid intervals.]

O FOR a closer walk with God, —
  A calm and heavenly frame ;
A light to shine upon the road
  That leads me to the Lamb.

2 Where is the blessedness I knew,
  When first I saw the Lord ?
Where is the soul-refreshing view
  Of Jesus and His word ?

3 What peaceful hours I once enjoy'd !
  How sweet their mem'ry still !
But they have left an aching void
  The world can never fill.

4 Return, O holy Dove, return,
  Sweet messenger of rest :
I hate the sins that made Thee mourn,
  And drove Thee from my breast.

5 The dearest idol I have known,
   Whate'er that idol be,
Help me to tear it from Thy throne,
   And worship only Thee.

6 So shall my walk be close with God,
   Calm and serene my frame;
So purer light shall mark the road
   That leads me to the Lamb.

70   *For Inward Peace.*   C. M.

O FOR a heart of calm repose
   Amid the world's loud roar,
A life that like a river flows
   Along a peaceful shore!

2 Come, Holy Spirit, still my heart
   With gentleness divine;
Indwelling peace Thou canst impart:
   O, make that blessing mine!

3 Above these scenes of storm and strife
   There spreads a region fair;
Give me to live that higher life,
   And breathe that heavenly air!

4 Come, Holy Spirit, breathe that peace!
   That victory make me win!
Then shall my soul her conflict cease,
   And find a heaven within.

71   *Thy Throne in my Heart.*   C. M.

[By CHARLES WESLEY.]

O FOR a heart to praise my God,
   A heart from sin set free ;
A heart that always feels Thy blood,
   So freely spilt for me : —

2 A heart resign'd, submissive, meek,
   My great Redeemer's throne ;
Where only Christ is heard to speak, —
   Where Jesus reigns alone.

3 O for a lowly, contrite heart,
   Believing, true, and clean ;
Which neither life nor death can part
   From Him that dwells within : —

4 A heart in every thought renew'd
   And full of love divine ;
Perfect, and right, and pure, and good,
   A copy, Lord, of Thine.

72   *Perfect Rest.*   L. M.

[By ANTON ULRICH, Duke of Brunswick, 1667. Translated from the German by Catherine Winkworth.]

O GOD, I long Thy light to see ;
   My God, I hourly think on Thee ;
O draw me up, nor hide Thy face,
But help me from Thy holy place.

2 Remember that I am Thy child ;
Forgive whate'er my soul defiled ;
Blot out my sins, that I may rise
Freely to Thee beyond the skies.

3 Help me to love the world no more;
Be master of my house and store;
The shield of faith around me throw,
And break the arrows of my foe.

4 Fain would my heart henceforward be
Fix'd, O my God, alone on Thee;
That heart and soul by Thee possest,
May find in Thee their perfect rest.

73   *Jacob's Prayer.*   C. M.

[By Rev. JOHN LOGAN, of Scotland ; died in 1788, aged 40.]

O GOD of Abram ! by whose hand
   Thy people still are fed —
Who, through this weary pilgrimage,
   Hast all our fathers led !

2 Our vows, our prayers, we now present
   Before Thy throne of grace :
God of our fathers, be the God
   Of their succeeding race.

3 Through each perplexing path of life
   Our wandering footsteps guide :
Give us each day our daily bread,
   And raiment fit provide !

4 O spread Thy covering wings around,
   Till all our wanderings cease,
And at our Father's loved abode
   Our feet arrive in peace !

74   *God, our Help.*   C. M.

[By Dr. WATTS. Paraphrase of Psalm 90.]

O GOD, our help in ages past,
   Our hope for years to come,

Our shelter from the stormy blast,
And our eternal home : —

2 Under the shadow of Thy throne
Still may we dwell secure;
Sufficient is Thine arm alone,
And our defense is sure.

3 Before the hills in order stood,
Or earth received her frame,
From everlasting Thou art God,
To endless years the same.

4 A thousand ages, in Thy sight,
Are like an evening gone ;
Short as the watch that ends the night,
Before the rising sun.

5 Time, like an ever-rolling stream,
Bears all its sons away ;
They fly, forgotten, as a dream
Dies at the opening day.

6 The busy tribes of flesh and blood,
With all their cares and fears,
Are carried downward by the flood,
And lost in foll'wing years.

7 O God, our help in ages past,
Our hope for years to come ;
Be Thou our guide while life shall last,
And our perpetual home !

75   *Fullness of Grace.*   L. M.
[By James Montgomery.]

O SPIRIT of the living God,
In all Thy plenitude of grace,

Where'er the foot of man hath trod,
Descend on our apostate race.

2 Give tongues of fire, and hearts of love,
To preach the reconciling word;
Give power and unction from above,
Where'er the joyful sound is heard.

3 Be darkness, at Thy coming, light;
Confusion — order, in Thy path;
Souls without strength, inspire with might;
Bid mercy triumph over wrath.

4 Baptize the nations; far and nigh
The triumphs of the cross record;
The name of Jesus glorify,
Till every kindred call Him Lord.

76 *Remember Me!* **C. M.**

[By Rev. THOMAS HOWEIS, M. D., of England; born 1732; died in 1820.]

O THOU from whom all goodness flows,
I lift my soul to Thee;
In all my sorrows, conflicts, woes,
O Lord, remember me.

2 When worn with pain, disease, and grief,
This feeble body see;
Grant patience, rest, and kind relief;
O Lord, remember me.

3 When, in the solemn hour of death,
I wait Thy just decree,
Be this the prayer of my last breath, —
O Lord, remember me.

4 And when before Thy throne I stand,
  And lift my soul to Thee,
  Then, with the saints at Thy right hand,
  O Lord, remember me.

77   *Bethel.*   L. M.

[By CHARLES WESLEY.]

O THOU, whom all Thy saints adore,
   We now with all Thy saints agree,
And bow our inmost souls before
  Thy glorious, awful Majesty.

2 We come, great God, to seek Thy face,
  And for Thy loving kindness wait;
  And O, how dreadful is this place !
  'Tis God's own house, 'tis heaven's gate.

3 Tremble our hearts to find Thee nigh;
  To Thee our trembling hearts aspire :
  And lo! we see descend from high
  The pillar and the flame of fire.

4 Still let it on th' assembly stay,
  And all the house with glory fill :
  To Canaan's bounds point out the way,
  And lead us to Thy holy hill.

5 There let us all with Jesus stand,
  And join the general Church above,
  And take our seats at Thy right hand,
  And sing Thine everlasting love.

78   *Pentecost.*   **L. M.**

[By HENRY MORE.]

ON all the earth Thy Spirit shower;
   The earth in righteousness renew;
Thy kingdom come, and hell's o'erpower,
   And to Thy sceptre all subdue.

2 Like mighty winds, or torrents fierce,
   Let Him opposers all o'errun;
And every law of sin reverse,
   That faith and love may make all one.

3 Yea, let Him, Lord, in every place
   His richest energy declare;
While lovely tempers, fruits of grace,
   The kingdom of Thy Christ prepare

4 Grant this, O holy God and true;
   The ancient seers thou didst inspire, -
To us perform the promise due, —
   Descend, and crown us now with fire

79   *Bless the Word!*   **C. M.**

[By Rev. JOSEPH HART, an English Independent; born in 1712; died 1768.

ONCE more we come before our God;
   Once more His blessing ask:
O may not duty seem a load,
   Nor worship prove a task.

2 Father, Thy quick'ning Spirit send
   From heaven, in Jesus' name,
And bid our waiting minds attend,
   And put our souls in frame.

3 May we receive the word we hear,
   Each in an honest heart;
   And keep the precious treasure there,
   And never with it part.

4 To seek Thee, all our hearts dispose;
   To each Thy blessings suit;
   And let the seed Thy servant sows,
   Produce abundant fruit.

80   *Rock of Ages.*   P. M.

[By Rev. Augustus M. Toplady, an English clergyman; born 1741; died in 1778. A favorite with every Christian who has ever heard it. Prince Albert used it in his dying hour. The author of "Rock of Ages," and the author of "Jesus lover of my Soul" were fierce polemics while they lived, carrying their warfare into personalities. They had zeal in prose but charity in poetry. Who doubts that either has failed to find a "refuge for his soul" in the "Rock of Ages?" Dr. Schaff notices as a curiosity that the Lyra Catholica has this hymn along-side hymns from the Breviary and Missal. We are one in Christ.]

ROCK of ages, cleft for me,
   Let me hide myself in Thee;
Let the water and the blood,
From Thy wounded side which flow'd,
Be of sin the double cure, —
Save from wrath and make me pure.

2 Not the labor of my hands
   Can fulfill Thy law's demands.
   Could my zeal no respite know,
   Could my tears forever flow, —
   These for sin could not atone;
   Thou must save, and Thou alone.

3 In my hand no price I bring,
   Simply to Thy cross I cling;
   Naked, come to Thee for dress;
   Helpless, look to Thee for grace;

Foul, I to the fountain hie, —
Wash me, Saviour, or I die.

4 While I draw this fleeting breath,
When my eyes shall close in death,
When I rise to worlds unknown,
And behold Thee on Thy throne, —
Rock of ages, cleft for me,
Let me hide myself in Thee.

81   *Litany.*   **P. M.**

By Sir ROBERT GRANT; born 1785; died 1838; Governor of Bombay. He
wrote twelve Sacred Lyrics, of which this is the best.]

SAVIOUR, when, in dust, to Thee
Low we bow th' adoring knee, —
When, repentant, to the skies
Scarce we lift our streaming eyes, —
O, by all Thy pain and woe
Suffer'd once for man below,
Bending from Thy throne on high,
Hear our solemn litany.

2 By Thine hour of dark despair,
By Thine agony of prayer;
By the cross, the nail, the thorn,
Piercing spear, and tort'ring scorn;
By the gloom that veil'd the skies
O'er the dreadful sacrifice, —
Listen to our humble cry,
Hear our solemn litany.

3 By Thy deep, expiring groan;
By the sad, sepulchral stone;
By the vault whose dark abode
Held in vain the rising God, —

O, from earth to heaven restored,
Mighty, re-ascended Lord,
Saviour, listen to our cry,
Hear our solemn litany.

82 *Sunday Evening.* **P. M.**

By SAMUEL F. SMITH, D. D., a Baptist clergyman of Massachusetts, born 1805.]

SOFTLY fades the twilight ray
Of the holy Sabbath day ;
Gently as life's setting sun,
When the Christian's course is run.

2 Night her solemn mantle spreads
O'er the earth, as daylight fades ;
All things tell of calm repose,
At the holy Sabbath's close.

3 Peace is on the world abroad ;
'Tis the holy peace of God, —
Symbol of the peace within,
When the spirit rests from sin.

4 Saviour, may our Sabbaths be
Days of peace and joy in Thee,
Till in heaven our souls repose,
Where the Sabbath ne'er shall close.

83 *Evening.* **P. M.**

By GEORGE W. DOANE, D. D., Protestant Episcopal Bishop of New Jersey ;
born in 1799, died in 1859.]

SOFTLY now the light of day
Fades upon our sight away ;
Free from care, from labor free,
Lord, we would commune with Thee.

2 Soon from us the light of day
   Shall forever pass away ;
   Then, from sin and sorrow free,
   Take us, Lord, to dwell with Thee.

84   *Sun of my Soul.*   **L. M.**

[By Rev. JOHN KEBLE, D. D., author of the " Christian Year ;" died 1866.]

SUN of my soul! Thou Saviour dear,
   It is not night if Thou be near:
O, may no earth-born cloud arise
To hide Thee from Thy servant's eyes!

2 When soft the dews of kindly sleep
   My wearied eyelids gently steep,
   Be my last thought, — how sweet to rest
   Forever on my Saviour's breast!

3 Abide with me from morn till eve,
   For without Thee I cannot live ;
   Abide with me when night is nigh,
   For without Thee I dare not die.

4 Be near to bless me when I wake,
   Ere through the world my way I take ;
   Abide with me till in Thy love
   I lose myself in heaven above.

85   *The Lord of Life.*   **L. M.**

[By OLIVER WENDELL HOLMES, M. D., born in 1809.]

SUN of our life! Thy wakening ray
   Sheds on our path the glow of day ;
Star of our hope! Thy soften'd light
Cheers the long watches of the night.

2 Our midnight is Thy smile withdrawn;
Our noontide is Thy gracious dawn;
Our rainbow's arch Thy mercy's sign;
All, save the clouds of sin, are Thine.

3 Lord of all life, below, above,
Whose light is truth, whose warmth is love;
Before Thy ever-blazing throne
We ask no lustre of our own.

4 Grant us Thy truth to make us free,
And kindling hearts that burn for Thee,
Till all Thy living altars claim
One holy light, one heavenly flame.

86 *Sabbath Joys.* **L. M.**
[By Dr. WATTS.]

SWEET is the work, my God, my King,
To praise Thy name, give thanks, and sing;
To show Thy love by morning light,
And talk of all Thy truth by night.

2 Sweet is the day of sacred rest;
No mortal cares shall seize my breast;
O may my heart in tune be found,
Like David's harp of solemn sound.

3 When grace has purified my heart,
Then I shall share a glorious part:
And fresh supplies of joy be shed,
Like holy oil to cheer my head.

4 Then shall I see, and hear, and know
All I desired or wish'd below;
And every power find sweet employ
In that eternal world of joy.

87   *" Thy face, Lord, will I seek."*   C. M.

[By CHARLES WESLEY.]

TALK with us, Lord, Thyself reveal,
    While here o'er earth we rove;
Speak to our hearts, and let us feel
The kindling of Thy love.

2 With Thee conversing, we forget
    All time, and toil, and care:
Labor is rest, and pain is sweet,
    If Thou, my God, art here.

3 Here then, my God, vouchsafe to stay,
    And bid my heart rejoice;
My bounding heart shall own Thy sway,
    And echo to Thy voice.

4 Thou callest me to seek Thy face; —
    'Tis all I wish to seek;
T' attend the whispers of Thy grace,
    And hear Thee inly speak.

5 Let this my every hour employ,
    Till I Thy glory see;
Enter into my Master's joy.
    And find my heaven in Thee.

88   *The Perfect Law.*   S. M.

[By CHARLES WESLEY.]

THE thing my God doth hate,
    That I no more may do;
Thy creature, Lord, again create,
    And all my soul renew.

2 That blessed law of Thine,
    Jesus, to me impart;

The Spirit's law of life divine,
O write it on my heart!

3 Implant it deep within,
Whence it may ne'er remove, —
The law of liberty from sin,
The perfect law of love.

4 Thy nature be my law, —
Thy spotless sanctity;
And sweetly every moment draw
My happy soul to Thee.

89 *Frailty of Life.* C. M.

[By Dr. WATTS.]

THEE we adore, eternal Name!
And humbly own to Thee
How feeble is our mortal frame —
What dying worms are we!

2 The year rolls round, and steals away
The breath that first it gave:
Whate'er we do, whate'er we be,
We're travelling to the grave.

3 Dangers stand thick through all the ground,
To push us to the tomb;
And fierce diseases wait around,
To hurry mortals home.

4 Waken, O Lord, our drowsy sense
To walk this dang'rous road;
And if our souls be hurried hence,
May they be found with God!

69

90   *The Endless Sabbath.*   **L. M.**

[By Dr. DODDRIDGE. Good taste suggests that the third stanza be not used
on a hot day in midsummer. It is more edifying in winter and on cloudy
afternoons.]

THINE earthly Sabbaths, Lord, we love ;
     But there's a nobler rest above :
To that our laboring souls aspire,
With ardent pangs of strong desire.

2 No more fatigue, no more distress ;
     Nor sin nor hell shall reach the place ;
No sighs shall mingle with the songs,
Which warble from immortal tongues.

3 No rude alarms of raging foes,
No cares to break the long repose,
No midnight shade, no clouded sun,
But sacred, high, eternal noon.

4 O long-expected day, begin,
Dawn on these realms of woe and sin :
Fain would we leave this weary road
And sleep in death, to rest with God.

91   *Exhaustless Love.*   **C. M.**

[By CHARLES WESLEY.]

THY ceaseless, unexhausted love,
     Unmerited and free,
Delights our evil to remove,
     And help our misery.

2 Thou waitest to be gracious still ;
     Thou dost with sinners bear ;
That, saved, we may Thy goodness feel,
     And all Thy grace declare.

3 Thy goodness and Thy truth to me,
  To every soul, abound;
  A vast, unfathomable sea,
  Where all our thoughts are drown'd.

4 Its streams the whole creation reach,
  So plenteous is the store;
  Enough for all, enough for each,
  Enough for evermore.

5 Faithful, O Lord, Thy mercies are, —
  A rock that cannot move:
  A thousand promises declare
  Thy constancy of love.

6 Throughout the universe it reigns,
  Unalterably sure;
  And while the truth of God remains,
  His goodness must endure.

92   *The Law of Christ.*   C. M.

[By CHARLES WESLEY.]

TRY us, O God, and search the ground
  Of every sinful heart:
Whate'er of sin in us is found,
  O bid it all depart.

2 If to the right or left we stray,
  Leave us not comfortless;
  But guide our feet into the way
  Of everlasting peace.

3 Help us to help each other, Lord,
  Each other's cross to bear:
  Let each his friendly aid afford,
  And feel his brother's care.

71

4 Help us to build each other up;
    Our little stock improve;
  Increase our faith, confirm our hope,
    And perfect us in love.

5 Up into Thee, our living Head,
    Let us in all things grow,
  Till Thou hast made us free indeed,
    And spotless here below.

6 Then, when the mighty work is wrought,
    Receive Thy ready bride:
  Give us in heaven a happy lot
    With all the sanctified.

93   *Sunday Morning.*   P. M.
          [By HEYWARD.]

WELCOME, delightful morn,
    Thou day of sacred rest;
  I hail thy kind return —
    Lord, make these moments blest:
  From the low train of mortal toys
  I soar to reach immortal joys.

2 Now may the King descend,
    And fill His throne of grace:
  Thy sceptre, Lord, extend,
    While saints address Thy face;
  Let sinners feel Thy quickening word,
  And learn to know and fear the Lord.

3 Descend, celestial Dove,
    With all Thy quickening powers;
  Disclose a Saviour's love,
    And bless the sacred hours:

Then shall my soul new life obtain,
Nor Sabbaths be indulged in vain.

94   *Welcome, Sweet Day.*   **S. M.**

[By Dr. WATTS.]

WELCOME, sweet day of rest,
    That saw the Lord arise :
Welcome to this reviving breast,
And these rejoicing eyes !

2 The King Himself comes near,
    And feasts His saints to-day ;
Here we may sit, and see Him here,
And love, and praise, and pray.

3 One day in such a place,
    Where Thou, my God, art seen,
Is sweeter than ten thousand days
Of pleasurable sin.

4 My willing soul would stay
    In such a frame as this,
And sit and sing herself away
To everlasting bliss.

95   *The Sacred Page.*   **C. M.**

[By WILLIAM COWPER.]

WHAT glory gilds the sacred page !
    Majestic, like the sun,
It gives a light to every age ;
It gives, but borrows none.

2 The power that gave it still supplies
    The gracious light and heat ;

Its truths upon the nations rise;
They rise, but never set.

3 Lord! everlasting thanks be Thine
For such a bright display,
As makes a world of darkness shine
With beams of heavenly day.

4 Our souls rejoicingly pursue
The steps of Him we love,
Till glory break upon our view
In brighter worlds above.

96   *All Thy Mercies.*   C. M

[By JOSEPH ADDISON.]

WHEN all Thy mercies, O my God,
My rising soul surveys,
Transported with the view, I'm lost
In wonder, love, and praise.

2 To all my weak complaints and cries,
Thy mercy lent an ear,
Ere yet my feeble thoughts had learn'd
To form themselves in prayer.

3 When in the slipp'ry paths of youth
With heedless steps, I ran;
Thine arm, unseen, convey'd me safe,
And led me up to man.

4 Through hidden dangers, toils, and deaths,
It gently clear'd my way; ·
And through the pleasing snares of vice,
More to be fear'd than they.

5 Through every period of my life
　Thy goodness I'll pursue;
And after death, in distant worlds,
　The pleasing theme renew.

6 Through all eternity to Thee
　A grateful song I'll raise;
But O! eternity's too short
　To utter all Thy praise.

97　　*The Wondrous Cross.*　　L. M.

[By Dr. WATTS.]

WHEN I survey the wondrous cross
　On which the Prince of glory died,
My richest gain I count but loss,
　And pour contempt on all my pride.

2 Forbid it, Lord, that I should boast,
　Save in the death of Christ, my God;
All the vain things that charm me most,
　I sacrifice them to His blood.

3 See, from His head, His hands, His feet,
　Sorrow and love flow mingled down:
Did e'er such love and sorrow meet,
　Or thorns compose so rich a crown?

4 Were the whole realm of nature mine,
　That were a present far too small;
. Love so amazing, so divine,
　Demands my soul, my life, my all.

98   *Resting on God.*   **C. M,**

[By Mrs. H. M. WILLIAMS. We know nothing of the author of this marvelously fine hymn, except her name, and that she was born 1762 and died 1827. Can any one change a solitary word in the fourth stanza without marring it?]

WHILE Thee I seek, protecting Power,
    Be my vain wishes still'd ;
And may this consecrated hour
    With better hopes be fill'd.

2 Thy love the power of thought bestow'd ;
    To Thee my thoughts would soar :
Thy mercy o'er my life has flow'd ;
    That mercy I adore.

3 In each event of life, how clear
    Thy ruling hand I see ;
Each blessing to my soul most dear,
    Because conferr'd by Thee.

4 In every joy that crowns my days,
    In every pain I bear,
My heart shall find delight in praise,
    Or seek relief in prayer.

5 When gladness wings my favor'd hour,
    Thy love my thoughts shall fill ;
Resign'd, when storms of sorrow lower,
    My soul shall meet Thy will.

6 My lifted eye, without a tear,
    The gath'ring storm shall see :
My steadfast heart shall know no fear ;
    That heart will rest on Thee.

99   *Heirs of Heaven.*   C. M.

[By Dr. WATTS.]

WHY should the children of a King
  Go mourning all their days?
Great Comforter, descend and bring
 The tokens of Thy grace.

2 Dost thou not dwell in all Thy saints,
 And seal the heirs of heaven?
When wilt Thou banish my complaints,
 And show my sins forgiven?

3 Assure my conscience of her part
 In the Redeemer's blood;
And bear Thy witness with my heart,
 That I am born of God.

4 Thou art the earnest of His love, —
 The pledge of joys to come;
May Thy blest wings, celestial Dove,
 Safely convey me home.

100   *Manifested in the Flesh.*   C. M.

[By CHARLES WESLEY.]

WITH glorious clouds encompass'd round,
  Whom angels dimly see,
Will the Unsearchable be found,
 Or God appear to me?

2 Will He forsake His throne above, —
 Himself to worms impart?
Answer, Thou Man of grief and love,
 And speak it to my heart.

3 In manifested love explain
  Thy wonderful design ;
What meant the suff'ring Son of man, —
The streaming blood divine ?

4 Didst Thou not in our flesh appear,
  And live and die below,
That I might now perceive Thee near,
  And my Redeemer know ?

5 Might view the Lamb in His own light,
  Whom angels dimly see ;
And gaze, transported at the sight,
  To all eternity ?

SPIRITUAL · SONGS.

---◆---

101   *Crown Him.*   **C. M.**

By Rev. EDWARD PERRONET, one of the associates of the Wesleys, afterwards with Lady Huntingdon, then a dissenting minister. In 1808 the
hymn was printed at Canterbury, Eng., on a card for the use of the Sun-
day-school to which is appended the following notice of the author:
"Rev. Edward Perronet died at Canterbury, January 2, 1792. His dying
words were 'Glory to God in the height of His divinity! Glory to God in
the depth of His humanity! Glory to God in His all-sufficiency! And
into His hands I commend my spirit.'"]

A LL hail the power of Jesus' name!
   Let angels prostrate fall;
Bring forth the royal diadem,
   And crown Him Lord of all.

2 Ye seed of Israel's chosen race,
   Ye ransom'd of the fall,
Hail Him who saves you by His grace,
   And crown Him Lord of all.

3 Sinners, whose love can ne'er forget
   The wormwood and the gall;
Go, spread your trophies at His feet,
   And crown Him Lord of all.

4 Let every tribe and every tongue
   That hear the Saviour's call,
Now shout in universal song,
   And crown Him Lord of all.

102   *Soldier of the Cross.*   C. M.
[By Dr. WATTS.]

A M I a soldier of the cross,
    A follower of the Lamb?
And shall I fear to own His cause,
    Or blush to speak His name!

2 Must I be carried to the skies
    On flowery beds of ease,
While others fought to win the prize,
    And sailed through bloody seas?

3 Are there no foes for me to face?
    Must I not stem the flood?
Is this vile world a friend to grace,
    To help me on to God?

4 Sure I must fight, if I would reign;
    Increase my courage, Lord;
I'll bear the toil, endure the pain,
    Supported by Thy word.

5 Thy saints, in all this glorious war,
    Shall conquer, though they die;
They view the triumph from afar;
    By faith they bring it nigh.

6 When that illustrious day shall rise,
    And all Thine armies shine
In robes of victory through the skies,
    The glory shall be Thine.

103   *Amazing Grace.*   C. M.
[By Rev. JOHN NEWTON.]

A MAZING grace! how sweet the sound!
    That saved a wretch like me:

I once was lost, but now am found,
  Was blind, but now I see.
2 'Twas grace that taught my heart to fear,
  And grace my fears relieved:
How precious did that grace appear
  The hour I first believed!
3 Through many dangers, toils, and snares,
  I have already come;
'Tis grace has brought me safe thus far,
  And grace will lead me home.
4 The Lord has promised good to me:
  His word my hope secures;
He will my shield and portion be
  As long as life endures.
5 Yea, when this heart and flesh shall fail,
  And mortal life shall cease,
I shall possess within the veil
  A life of joy and peace.

104   *Meeting, after Absence.*   S. M.
        [By CHARLES WESLEY.]

AND are we yet alive!—
  And see each other's face!—
Glory and praise to Jesus give,
  For His redeeming grace.
Preserved by power divine
  To full salvation here, ·
Again in Jesus' praise we join,
  And in His sight appear.
2 What troubles have we seen!
  What conflicts have we passed!

Fightings without, and fears within,
　　Since we assembled last!
But out of all the Lord
　　Hath brought us by His love;
And still He doth His help afford,
　　And hides our life above.

3 Then let us make our boast
　　Of His redeeming power,
Which saves us to the uttermost,
　　Till we can sin no more:
Let us take up the cross,
　　Till we the crown obtain;
And gladly reckon all things loss,
　　So we may Jesus gain.

105　　*The Joyous Prospect.*　　**C. M.**

[By Charles Wesley.]

AND let this feeble body fail,
　　And let it faint or die;
My soul shall quit the mournful vale,
　　And soar to worlds on high;
Shall join the disembodied saints,
　　And find its long-sought rest,—
That only bliss for which it pants,
　　In the Redeemer's breast.

2 In hope of that immortal crown
　　I now the cross sustain,
And gladly wander up and down,
　　And smile at toil and pain:
I suffer on my threescore years,
　　Till my Deliv'rer come,

And wipe away His servant's tears,
And take His exile home.

3 O what hath Jesus bought for me!
Before my ravish'd eyes
Rivers of life divine I see,
And trees of Paradise:
I see a world of spirits bright,
Who taste the pleasures there;
They all are robed in spotless white,
And conqu'ring palms they bear.

4 O what are all my suff'rings here,
If, Lord, Thou count me meet
With that enraptured host t' appear,
And worship at Thy feet!
Give joy or grief, give ease or pain:
Take life or friends away,
But let me find them all again
In that eternal day.

106   *Sunday Morning.*   L. M.
[By SAMUEL STENNETT, D. D., an English Baptist.]

A NOTHER six days' work is done;
Another Sabbath is begun:
Return, my soul, unto thy rest;
Enjoy the day Thy God hath blest.

2 O that my thoughts and thanks may rise,
As grateful incense to the skies!
And draw from heaven that calm repose
Which none but he who feels it knows;

3 That heavenly calm within the breast!
It is the pledge of that dear rest

Which for the church of God remains, —
The end of cares, the end of pains.

4 In holy duties let the day,
In holy pleasures, pass away.
How sweet a Sabbath thus to spend,
In hope of one that ne'er shall end!

107   *The Mercy-seat.*   **C. M.**

[By Rev. JOHN NEWTON, in 1779.]

APPROACH, my soul, the mercy-seat
Where Jesus answers prayer;
There humbly fall before His feet,
For none can perish there.

2 Thy promise is my only plea,
With this I venture nigh;
Thou callest burdened souls to Thee,
And such, O Lord, am I.

3 Bowed down beneath a load of sin,
By Satan sorely prest,
By war without and fears within,
I come to Thee for rest.

4 Be Thou my shield and hiding-place,
That, sheltered near Thy side,
I may my fierce accuser face,
And tell Him, Thou hast died!

5 O wondrous love! to bleed and die,
To bear the cross and shame,
That guilty sinners, such as I,
Might plead Thy gracious name!

6 " Poor, tempest-tosséd soul be still,
My promised grace receive: "

'Tis Jesus speaks! I must, I will,
I can, I do believe.

108　　　　　*Abba, Father.*　　　**P. M.**

[By CHARLES WESLEY.]

ARISE, my soul, arise;
　Shake off thy guilty fears;
The bleeding Sacrifice
　In my behalf appears:
Before the throne my Surety stands,
My name is written on his Hands.

2 He ever lives above,
　For me to intercede;
His all-redeeming love,
　His precious blood, to plead;
His blood atoned for all our race,
And sprinkles now the throne of grace.

3 Five bleeding wounds He bears,
　Received on Calvary;
They pour effectual prayers,
　They strongly plead for me:
Forgive him, O forgive, they cry,
Nor let that ransom'd sinner die.

4 The Father hears Him pray,
　His dear anointed One:
He cannot turn away
　The presence of His Son:
His Spirit answers to the blood,
And tells me I am born of God.

5 My God is reconciled;
　His pard'ning voice I hear:

He owns me for His child ;
I can no longer fear : —
With confidence I now draw nigh,
And Father, Abba, Father, cry.

109   *The Song of the Lamb.*   **C. M.**

[By WILLIAM HAMMOND, a Calvinistic-Methodist preacher, afterwards
a Moravian ; died 1783.]

Rev. xv. 3. 4.

A WAKE, and sing the song
Of Moses and the Lamb!
Wake, every heart, and every tongue,
To praise the Saviour's name!

2 Sing of His dying love ;
Sing of His rising power :
Sing how He intercedes above,
For those whose sins He bore.

3 Sing, till we feel our hearts
Ascending with our tongues ;
Sing, till the love of sin departs,
And grace inspires our songs.

4 Sing on your heavenly way,
Ye ransomed sinners, sing!
Sing on, rejoicing every day
In Christ, th' exalted King.

5 Soon shall we hear Him say,
" Ye blessed children, come! "
Soon will He call us hence away
To our eternal home.

6 Soon shall our raptured tongue
His endless praise proclaim,
And sweeter voices tune the song
Of Moses and the Lamb.

110   *Away with Fear.*   L. M.

[By CHARLES WESLEY. A paraphrase of Habakkuk iii. 17, 18.]

AWAY, my unbelieving fear,
   Fear shall in me no more have place;
My Saviour doth not yet appear, —
   He hides the brightness of His face:
But shall I therefore let Him go,
   And basely to the tempter yield?
No, in the strength of Jesus, no,
   I never will give up my shield.

2 Although the vine its fruit deny,
   Although the olive yield no oil,
The with'ring fig-trees droop and die,
   The fields elude the tiller's toil, —
The empty stall no herd afford,
   And perish all the bleating race,
Yet will I triumph in the Lord, —
   The God of my salvation praise.

111   *The New Song.*   C. M.

[By Dr. WATTS. Paraphrase of Rev. v.]

BEHOLD the glories of the Lamb,
   Amid His Father's throne;
Prepare new honors for His name,
   And songs before unknown.

2 Let elders worship at His feet,
   The Church adore around,
With vials full of odors sweet,
   And harps of sweeter sound.

3 Those are the prayers of all the saints,
   And these the hymns they raise:

Jesus is kind to our complaints;
He loves to hear our praise.

4 He has redeemed our souls with blood,
Has broken every chain,
Has made us kings and priests to God,
And we with Him shall reign.

112   *Christian Sympathy.*   **S. M.**

[By Rev. John Fawcett, D. D., born in 1750; died in 1817. He was pastor of a poor Church in Yorkshire. The size of family led him to accept the call of a Baptist Church in London, but while the last of the wagons that were to transport his furniture was being packed, his poor people clung to him with tears and lamentings, that so moved him as to induce him to remain. This gave origin to this hymn of mutual love, which has been sung by thousands of Christians. George III. made him offers of preferment, but he answered substantially that he " dwelt among his own people and needed nothing that even a King could bestow." He died in the pulpit while preaching to an immense congregation on the text, " I am this day going the way of all the earth." Joshua xxiii. 14.]

BLEST be the tie that binds
Our hearts in Christian love;
The fellowship of kindred minds
Is like to that above.

2 Before our Father's throne
We pour our ardent prayers;
Our fears, our hopes, our aims are one, —
Our comforts and our cares.

3 We share our mutual woes;
Our mutual burdens bear;
And often for each other flows
The sympathizing tear.

4 When we asunder part,
It gives us inward pain;
But we shall still be join'd in heart,
And hope to meet again.

5 This glorious hope revives
  Our courage by the way;
While each in expectation lives,
  And longs to see the day.
6 From sorrow, toil, and pain,
  And sin we shall be free;
And perfect love and friendship reign
  Through all eternity.

113   *The Year of Jubilee.*   P. M.
                  [By CHARLES WESLEY.]

BLOW ye the trumpet, blow
    The gladly solemn sound;
Let all the nations know,
    To earth's remotest bound,
The year of jubilee is come;
Return, ye ransom'd sinners, home.

2 Jesus, our great High-Priest,
    Hath full atonement made:
Ye weary spirits, rest;
    Ye mournful souls, be glad;
The year of jubilee is come;
Return, ye ransom'd sinners, home.

3 Extol the Lamb of God, —
    The all-atoning Lamb;
Redemption in His blood
    Throughout the world proclaim:
The year of jubilee is come;
Return, ye ransomed sinners, home.

4 Ye slaves of sin and hell,
    Your liberty receive,

And safe in Jesus dwell,
   And blest in Jesus live :
The year of jublilee is come ;
Return, ye ransom'd sinners, home.

114   *Breast the Wave, Christian.*   **P. M.**

BREAST the wave, Christian, when it is
   strongest ;
Watch for day, Christian, when night is longest;
Onward and onward still be thine endeavor ;
The rest that remaineth, endureth forever.

2 Fight the fight, Christian ; Jesus is o'er thee ;
Run the race, Christian ; heaven is before thee :
He who hath promisèd faltereth never ;
O, trust in the love that endureth forever.

3 Lift the eye, Christian, just as it closeth :
Raise the heart, Christian, ere it reposeth :
Nothing thy soul from the Saviour shall sever ;
Then shalt thou mount upward to praise Him
   forever.

115   *The Pilgrim's Song.*   **P. M.**

[By Rev. JOHN CENNICK, an English Moravian of the last century.]

CHILDREN of the heavenly King,
   As we journey let us sing ;
Sing our Saviour's worthy praise,
Glorious in His works and ways.

2 We are trav'ling home to God,
In the way our fathers trod ;
They are happy now, and we
Soon their happiness shall see.

3 O ye banish'd seed, be glad;
   Christ our Advocate is made:
   Us to save our flesh assumes, —
   Brother to our souls becomes.

4 Fear not, brethren, joyful stand
   On the borders of our land;
   Jesus Christ, our Father's Son,
   Bids us undismay'd go on.

5 Lord! obediently we'll go,
   · Gladly leaving all below:
   Only Thou our leader be,
   And we still will follow Thee.

116   *The Resolution.*   C. M.

[By Rev. EDMUND JONES, a popular Welsh Baptist minister of the last century.]

COME, humble sinner, in whose breast
   A thousand thoughts revolve,
Come, with your guilt and fear oppress'd,
   And make this last resolve:

2 I'll go to Jesus, though my sins
   Like mountains round me close;
   I know His courts, I'll enter in,
   Whatever may oppose.

3 Prostrate I'll lie before His throne,
   And there my guilt confess;
   I'll tell Him, I'm a wretch undone
   Without His sov'reign grace.

4 Perhaps He will admit my plea,
   Perhaps will hear my prayer;
   But, if I perish, I will pray,
   And perish only there.

5 I can but perish if I go —
   I am resolved to try;
For if I stay away, I know
   I must forever die.

6 But if I die with mercy sought,
   When I the King have tried
This were to die, delightful thought!
   As sinner never died.

117   *Bliss-inspiring Hope.*   **P. M.**
        [By CHARLES WESLEY.]

COME on, my partners in distress,
  My comrades through the wilderness,
Who still your bodies feel:
Awhile forget your griefs and fears,
And look beyond this vale of tears,
   To that celestial hill.

2 Beyond the bounds of time and space,
Look forward to that heavenly place,
   The saints' secure abode;
On faith's strong eagle pinions rise,
And force your passage to the skies,
   And scale the mount of God.

3 Who suffer with our Master here,
We shall before His face appear,
   And by His side sit down;
To patient faith the prize is sure;
And all that to the end endure   ·
   The cross, shall wear the crown.

4 Thrice blessed, bliss-inspiring hope!
It lifts the fainting spirits up;

It brings to life the dead:
Our conflicts here shall soon be past,
And you and I ascend at last,
Triumphant with our Head.

5 That great mysterious Deity
We soon with open face shall see;
The beatific sight
Shall fill the heavenly courts with praise,
And wide diffuse the golden blaze
Of everlasting light.

118   *Come, ye Disconsolate.*   P. M.

[By THOMAS MOORE, born in Ireland 1780; died in 1852.]

COME, ye disconsolate, where'er ye languish;
  Come to the mercy-seat, fervently kneel;
Here bring your wounded hearts, here tell your
    anguish;
Earth has no sorrow that Heaven cannot heal.

2 Joy of the desolate, light of the straying,
  Hope of the penitent, fadeless and pure, —
Here speaks the Comforter, tenderly saying, —
Earth has no sorrow that Heaven cannot cure.

3 Here see the bread of life; see waters flowing
  Forth from the throne of God, pure from above;
Come to the feast of love; come, ever knowing —
Earth has no sorrow but Heaven can remove.

119   *Glory begun Below.*   S. M.

[By Dr. WATTS. Improved by JOHN WESLEY.]

COME, ye that love the Lord,
  And let your joys be known;

Join in a song with sweet accord,
  While ye surround His throne.

2 The sorrows of the mind
  Be banished from this place,
Religion never was designed
  To make our pleasures less.

3 Let those refuse to sing
  Who never knew our God,
But servants of the heavenly King
  May speak their joys abroad.

4 The God that rules on high,
  That all the earth surveys,
That rides upon the stormy sky,
  And calms the roaring seas;

5 This awful God is ours,
  Our Father and our love;
He will send down His heavenly powers,
  To carry us above.

PART II.

1 There we shall see His face,
  And never, never sin:
There, from the rivers of His grace,
  Drink endless pleasures in;

2 Yea, and before we rise
  To that immortal state,
The thoughts of such amazing bliss
  Should constant joys create.

3 The men of grace have found
  Glory begun below:

Celestial fruit on earthly ground
From faith and hope may grow.

4 The hill of Zion yields
A thousand sacred sweets,
Before we reach the heavenly fields
Or walk the golden streets.

5 Then let our songs abound,
And every tear be dry:
We're marching through Immanuel's ground,
To fairer worlds on high.

120   *The Invitation.*   **P. M.**

[By Rev. JOSEPH HART, an English Independent, born 1712 ; died 1768.

COME, ye sinners, poor and needy,
    Weak and wounded, sick and sore;
Jesus ready stands to save you,
    Full of pity, love, and power:
        He is able,
    He is willing : doubt no more.

2 Now, ye needy, come and welcome;
    God's free bounty glorify;
True belief and true repentance, —
    Every grace that brings you nigh, —
        Without money,
    Come to Jesus Christ and buy.

3 Let not conscience make you linger:
    Nor of fitness fondly dream :
All the fitness He requireth
    Is to feel your need of Him:
        This he gives you, —
    'Tis the Spirit's glimm'ring beam.

4 Come, ye weary, heavy laden,
    Bruised and mangled by the fall;
If you tarry till you're better,
    You will never come at all;
        Not the righteous, —
    Sinners Jesus came to call.

5 Agonizing in the garden,
    Your Redeemer prostrate lies;
On the bloody tree behold Him!
    Hear Him cry, before He dies,
        It is finish'd! —
    Sinners, will not this suffice?

6 Lo! th' incarnate God, ascending,
    Pleads the merit of His blood:
Venture on Him, — venture freely;
    Let no other trust intrude:
        None but Jesus
    Can do helpless sinners good.

7 Saints and angels, join'd in concert,
    Sing the praises of the Lamb;
While the blissful seats of heaven
    Sweetly echo with His name:
        Hallelujah!
    Sinners here may do the same.

121   *Daughter of Zion!*   P. M.

DAUGHTER of Zion! awake from thy sadness:
    Awake, for thy foes shall oppress thee no more;
Bright o'er thy hills dawns the day-star of gladness;
    Arise! for the night of thy sorrow is o'er.

2 Strong were thy foes, but the arm that sub-
     dued them,
And scattered their legions, was mightier far;
They fled, like the chaff, from the scourge that
     pursued them ;
For vain were their steeds and their chariots
     of war !

3 Daughter of Zion ! the power that hath saved
     thee,
Extolled with the harp and the timbrel should
     be :
Shout! for the foe is destroyed that enslaved
     thee,
Th' oppressor is vanquished, and Zion is free !

122   *Depth of Mercy !*   P. M.
          [By CHARLES WESLEY.]

DEPTH of mercy ! can there be
     Mercy still reserved for me ?
Can my God His wrath forbear ?
Me, the chief of sinners, spare ?

2 I have long withstood His grace ;
Long provoked Him to His face ;
Would not hearken to His calls ;
Grieved Him by a thousand falls.

3 Now incline me to repent ;
Let me now my sins lament ;
Now my foul revolt deplore,
Weep, believe, and sin no more. •

4 Kindled His relentings are ;
Me He now delights to spare ;

Cries, How shall I give thee up?—
Lets the lifted thunder drop.

5 There for me the Saviour stands;
Shows His wounds, and spreads His hands;
God is love! I know, I feel;
Jesus weeps, and loves me still.

123   *The Mercy-seat.*   **L. M.**

[By STOWELL.]

FROM every stormy wind that blows,
 From every swelling tide of woes,
There is a calm, a sure retreat;
'Tis found beneath the mercy-seat.

2 There is a place, where Jesus sheds
The oil of gladness on our heads;
A place than all besides more sweet,—
It is the blood-bought mercy-seat.

3 There is a scene, where spirits blend,
Where friend holds fellowship with friend;
Though sunder'd far, by faith they meet
Around one common mercy-seat.

4 Ah! whither could we flee for aid,
When tempted, desolate, dismay'd?
Or how the hosts of hell defeat,
Had suff'ring saints no mercy-seat?

5 There, there on eagles' wings we soar,
And sin and sense molest no more;
And heaven comes down our souls to greet,
While glory crowns the mercy-seat.

6 My cunning hand shall lose its skill,
My glowing tongue be cold and still,
My bounding heart forget to beat
Ere I forget the mercy-seat.

124 .   *Missionary Hymn.*   P. M.

[By Bishop HEBER.]

FROM Greenland's icy mountains,
  From India's coral strand;
Where Afric's sunny fountains
  Roll down their golden sand;
From many an ancient river,
  From many a palmy plain,
They call us to deliver
  Their land from error's chain.

2 What though the spicy breezes
    Blow soft o'er Ceylon's isle:
  Though every prospect pleases,
    And only man is vile:
  In vain with lavish kindness
    The gifts of God are strown;
  The heathen in his blindness
    Bows down to wood and stone.

3 Shall we, whose souls are lighted
    With wisdom from on high,
  Shall we to men benighted
    The lamp of life deny?
  Salvation! — O salvation!
    The joyful sound proclaim,
  Till earth's remotest nation
    Has learn'd Messiah's name.

99

4 Waft, waft, ye winds, his story,
   And you, ye waters, roll,
Till, like a sea of glory,
   It spread from pole to pole:
Till o'er our ransom'd nature
   The Lamb for sinners slain,
Redeemer, King, Creator,
   In bliss return to reign.

125   *The Cloud of Witnesses.*   **C M.**

[By Dr. WATTS.]

GIVE me the wings of faith, to rise
   Within the veil, and see
The saints above — how great their joys,
   How bright their glories be!

2 Once they were mourning here below,
   And wet their couch with tears;
They wrestled hard, as we do now,
   With sins and doubts and fears.

3 I ask them whence their victory came;
   They, with united breath,
Ascribe their conquest to the Lamb,
   Their triumph to His death.

4 Our glorious Leader claims our praise
   For his own pattern given,
While the long cloud of witnesses
   Show the same path to heaven.

126   *Be not Afraid.*   S. M.

[Translated from the German of Rev. PAUL GERHARD by Rev. John Wesley.]

GIVE to the winds thy fears;
    Hope, and be undismay'd;
·God hears thy sighs and counts thy tears;
    God shall lift up thy head;
Through waves, and clouds, and storms,
    He gently clears thy way;
Wait thou His time, so shall this night
    Soon end in joyous day.

2 Still heavy is thy heart?
    Still sink thy spirits down?
Cast off the weight, — let fear depart,
    And every care be gone.
What though thou rulest not;
    Yet heaven, and earth, and hell,
Proclaim, — God sitteth on the throne,
    And ruleth all things well.

3 Leave to His sov'reign sway
    To choose and to command:
So shalt thou, wond'ring, own His way,
    How wise, how strong His hand!
Far, far above thy thought
    His counsel shall appear,
When fully He the work hath wrought
    That caused thy needless fear.

127   *Grace All-sufficient.*   S. M.

[By Dr. DODDRIDGE.]

GRACE! 'tis a charming sound,
    Harmonious to the ear;

Heaven with the echo shall resound,
And all the earth shall hear.

2 Grace first contrived a way
To save rebellious man ;
And all the steps that grace display
Which drew the wondrous plan.

3 Grace taught my roving feet
To tread the heavenly road ;
And new supplies each hour I meet,
While pressing on to God.

4 Grace all the work shall crown,
Through everlasting days ;
It lays in heaven the topmost stone,
And well deserves our praise.

128   *" Lovest Thou Me ? "*   P. M.
[By WILLIAM COWPER.]

HARK, my soul, it is the Lord ;
'Tis thy Saviour, — hear His word,
Jesus speaks, He speaks to thee :
" Say, poor sinner, lov'st thou me ?

2 " I delivered thee when bound,
And when wounded heal'd thy wound,
Sought thee wandering, set thee right,
Turn'd thy darkness into light.

3 " Can a woman's tender care
Cease toward the child she bare ?
Yes, *she* may forgetful be,
Yet will *I* remember thee.

4 " Mine is an unchanging love,
Higher than the heights above,

Deeper than the depths beneath,
Free and faithful, strong as death.

5 " Thou shalt see my glory soon,
When the work of grace is done;
Partner of my throne shall be :
Say, poor sinner, lov'st thou me ? "

6 Lord, it is my chief complaint
That my love is still so faint,
Yet I love Thee and adore :
O for grace to love Thee more !

129   .   *Christ's Kingdom.*   **P. M.**

[By JAMES MONTGOMERY. Paraphrase of Psalm 72.]

HAIL to the Lord's anointed,
Great David's greater Son !
Hail, in the time appointed,
His reign on earth begun !
He comes to break oppression, —
To set the captive free ;
To take away trangression,
And rule in equity.

2 He comes, with succor speedy,
To those who suffer wrong ;
To help the poor and needy,
And bid the weak be strong ;
To give them songs for sighing, —
Their darkness turn to light, —
Whose souls, condemn'd and dying,
Were precious in His sight.

3 He shall descend like showers
Upon the fruitful earth,

And love and joy, like flowers,
　　Spring in His path to birth:
Before Him, on the mountains,
　　Shall Peace, the herald, go,
And righteousness, in fountains,
　　From hill to valley flow.

4 To Him shall prayer unceasing,
　　And daily vows ascend;
His kingdom still increasing, —
　　A kingdom without end:
The tide of time shall never
　　His covenant remove;　　•
His name shall stand forever;
　　That name to us is Love.

130　　　　　*" Christ is Born."*　　　　**P. M.**
[By CHARLES WESLEY.]

HARK! the herald angels sing,
　　" Glory to the new-born King!
Peace on earth, and mercy mild;
God and sinners reconciled."

2 Joyful, all ye nations, rise;
Join the triumphs of the skies;
With th' angelic hosts proclaim,
" Christ is born in Bethlehem."

3 Mild He lays His glory by;
Born that man no more may die;
Born to raise the sons of earth;
Born to give them second birth.

4 Let us, then, with angels sing,
" Glory to the new-born King! —

Peace on earth, and mercy mild;
God and sinners reconciled ! "

131   *The Song of Jubilee.*   P. M.

[By JAMES MONTGOMERY.]

HARK ! the song of jubilee ;
    Loud as mighty thunders roar,
Or the fullness of the sea,
    When it breaks upon the shore :
Hallelujah ! for the Lord
    God omnipotent shall reign ;
Hallelujah ! let the word
    Echo round the earth and main.

2 Hallelujah ! — hark ! the sound,
    From the centre to the skies,
Wakes above, beneath, around,
    All creation's harmonies :
See Jehovah's banners furl'd ;
    Sheath'd His sword : He speaks —'tis done,
And the kingdoms of this world
    Are the kingdoms of His Son.

3 He shall reign from pole to pole
    With illimitable sway ;
He shall reign, when, like a scroll,
    Yonder heavens have pass'd away :
Then the end ; — beneath His rod,
    Man's last enemy shall fall ;
Hallelujah ! Christ in God,
    God in Christ, is all in all.

132 *Jesus Reigns.* P. M.

[By Rev. THOMAS KELLY, a popular Irish preacher, born 1769; died in 1855.]

HARK! ten thousand harps and voices
    Sound the note of praise above:
Jesus reigns, and heaven rejoices:
    Jesus reigns, the God of love:
See, He sits on yonder throne:
Jesus rules the world alone.

2 Jesus, hail! whose glory brightens
    All above, and gives it worth:
Lord of life, Thy smile enlightens,
    Cheers, and charms Thy saints on earth:
When we think of love like Thine,
Lord, we own it love divine.

3 King of glory, reign forever:
    Thine an everlasting crown:
Nothing from Thy love shall sever
    Those whom Thou hast made Thine own:
Happy objects of Thy grace,
Destined to behold Thy face.

4 Saviour, hasten Thine appearing:
    Bring, O bring the glorious day,
When, the joyful summons hearing,
    Heaven and earth shall pass away:
Then, with golden harps, we'll sing,
" Glory, glory to our King!"

133   *Leading Captivity Captive.*   **L. M.**

[By Dr. WATTS. In most versions the first line is given, " He dies ! the
Friend of sinners dies ! " In this, the original line of Watts is restored.
All other deviations from the original are by John Wesley, probably the
most judicious *mender* of hymns the Church has produced.]

HE dies! the Heavenly Lover dies!
   Lo! Salem's daughters weep around :
A solemn darkness veils the skies,
   A sudden trembling shakes the ground :
Come, saints, and drop a tear or two
   For Him who groan'd beneath your load ;
He shed a thousand drops for you, —
   A thousand drops of richest blood.

2 Here's love and grief beyond degree :
   The Lord of glory dies for man !
But lo ! what sudden joys we see :
   Jesus, the dead, revives again.
The rising God forsakes the tomb ;
   In vain the tomb forbids His rise ;
Cherubic legions guard Him home,
   And shout Him welcome to the skies.

3 Break off your tears, ye saints, and tell
   How high your great Deliv'rer reigns ;
Sing how He spoil'd the hosts of hell,
   And led the monster Death in chains :
Say, Live forever, wondrous King !
   Born to redeem, and strong to save ;
Then ask the monster, Where's thy sting ?
   And, Where's thy vict'ry, boasting Grave ?

8

134   *" That Blessed Hope."*   **P. M.**

[By CHARLES WESLEY.]

HEAD of the Church triumphant,
    We joyfully adore Thee ;
Till Thou appear, Thy members here
    Shall sing like those in glory:
We lift our hearts and voices
    With blest anticipation ;
And cry aloud, and give to God
    The praise of our salvation.

2 Thou dost conduct Thy people
    Through torrents of temptation ;
Nor will we fear, while Thou art near,
    The fire of tribulation :
The world, with sin and Satan,
    In vain our march opposes ;
By Thee we shall break through them all,
    And sing the song of Moses.

3 By faith we see the glory
    To which Thou shalt restore us ;
The cross despise for that high prize
    Which Thou hast set before us :
And if Thou count us worthy,
    We each, as dying Stephen,
Shall see Thee stand at God's right hand,
    To take us up to heaven.

135   *Precious Promises.*   **P. M.**

[By Rev. JOHN KIRKHAM, an early English Methodist. This hymn first
appeared in Rippon's Selection in 1787.]

HOW firm a foundation, ye saints of the Lord,
    Is laid for your faith in His excellent word!

What more can He say than to you He hath said,
You who unto Jesus for refuge have fled?

2 " Fear not: I am with thee: O be not dis-
    may'd !
I, I am thy God, and will still give thee aid:
I'll strengthen thee, help thee, and cause thee to
    stand,
Upheld by my righteous, omnipotent hand.

3 " When through the deep waters I call thee to
    go,
The rivers of woe shall not thee overflow ;
For I will be with thee, thy troubles to bless,
And sanctify to thee thy deepest distress.

4 " When through fiery trials thy pathway shall
    lie,
My grace, all sufficient, shall be thy supply :
The flame shall not hurt thee : I only design
Thy dross to consume, and thy gold to refine.

5 " E'en down to old age, all my people shall
    prove
My sovereign, eternal, unchangeable love ;
And when hoary hairs shall their temples adorn,
Like lambs they shall still in my bosom be borne.

6 " The soul that on Jesus still leans for repose.
I *will* not, I *will* not desert to his foes :
That soul, though all hell should endeavor to
    shake,
I'll never, *no never*, NO NEVER forsake."

136   *Assurance of Hope.*   C, M
             [By CHARLES WESLEY.]

HOW happy every child of grace,
       Who knows his sins forgiven!
This earth, he cries, is not my place;
    I seek my place in heaven:
A country far from mortal sight,
    Yet O, by faith I see;
The land of rest, the saints' delight, —
    The heaven prepared for me.

2 O what a blessed hope is ours!
    While here on earth we stay,
We more than taste the heavenly powers,
    And antedate that day:
We feel the resurrection near, —
    Our life in Christ conceal'd, —
And with His glorious presence here
    Our earthen vessels fill'd.

3 O would He more of heaven bestow!
    And when the vessels break,
Let our triumphant spirits go
    To grasp the God we seek;
In rapturous awe on Him to gaze,
    Who bought the sight for me;
And shout and wonder at His grace
    To all eternity.

137   *The Pilgrim's Lot.*   P. M,
             [By Rev. JOHN WESLEY.]

HOW happy is the pilgrim's lot;
       How free from every anxious thought,

From worldly hope and fear!
Confined to neither court nor cell,
His soul disdains on earth to dwell,
He only sojourns here.

2 This happiness in part is mine,
Already saved from low design,
From every creature-love;
Blest with the scorn of finite good;
My soul is lighten'd of its load,
And seeks the things above.

3 There is my house and portion fair;
My treasure and my heart are there,
And my abiding home;
For me my elder brethren stay,
And angels beckon me away,
And Jesus bids me come.

4 I come, Thy servant, Lord, replies;
I come to meet Thee in the skies,
And claim my heavenly rest!
Soon will the pilgrim's journey end;
Then, O my Saviour, Brother, Friend,
Receive me to Thy breast!

138   *Sufficiency of Jesus.*   **P. M**
By Rev. JOHN NEWTON.]

HOW tedious and tasteless the hours
    When Jesus no longer I see!
Sweet prospects, sweet birds, and sweet flowers
    Have all lost their sweetness to me;
The midsummer sun shines but dim,
    The fields strive in vain to look gay;

But when I am happy in Him,
  December 's as pleasant as May.

2 His name yields the richest perfume,
    And sweeter than music His voice;
  His presence disperses my gloom,
    And makes all within me rejoice;
  I should, were He always thus nigh,
    Have nothing to wish or to fear;
  No mortal so happy as I, —
    My summer would last all the year.

3 Content with beholding His face,
    My all to His pleasure resign'd,
  No changes of season or place
    Would make any change in my mind:
  While blest with a sense of His love,
    A palace a toy would appear;
  And prisons would palaces prove,
    If Jesus would dwell with me there.

4 Dear Lord, if indeed I am Thine,
    If Thou art my sun and my song,
  Say, why do I languish and pine?
    And why are my winters so long?
  O drive these dark clouds from my sky;
    Thy soul-cheering presence restore;
  Or take me to Thee up on high,
    Where winter and clouds are no more.

139   *" I heard the Voice of Jesus."*   C. M.

'By HORATIUS BONAR, D. D., of the Free Church of Scotland, born 1808.
This hymn written in 1856.]

I HEARD the voice of Jesus say,
  " Come unto me and rest;

Lay down, thou weary one, lay down
  Thy head upon my breast:"
I came to Jesus as I was,
  Weary, and worn, and sad;
I found in Him a resting-place,
  And He has made me glad.

2 I heard the voice of Jesus say,
  " Behold, I freely give
The living-water! thirsty one,
  Stoop down, and drink, and live."
I came to Jesus, and I drank
  Of that life-giving stream:
My thirst was quenched, my soul revived,
  And now I live in Him.

3 I heard the voice of Jesus say,
  " I am this dark world's light:
Look unto me; thy morn shall rise,
  And all thy day be bright."
I looked to Jesus, and I found
  In Him my Star, my Sun;
And in that light of life I'll walk
  Till all my journey 's done.

140   " *He hath borne our Griefs.*"   P. M.
      [By Dr. BONAR. Suggested by Isa. liii. 4.]

I LAY my sins on Jesus,
  The spotless Lamb of God;
He bears them all and frees us
  From the accursed load:
I bring my guilt to Jesus,
  To wash my crimson stains

White in His blood most precious,
Till not a stain remains.

2 I lay my wants on Jesus;
　All fullness dwells in Him;
He heals all my diseases,
　He doth my soul redeem:
I lay my griefs on Jesus,
　My burdens and my cares;
He from them all releases,
　He all my sorrow shares.

3 I rest my soul on Jesus,
　This weary soul of mine;
His right hand me embraces,
　I on His breast recline.
I love the name of Jesus,
　Immanuel, Christ, the Lord;
Like fragrance on the breezes,
　His name abroad is poured.

141　　　*Everlasting Praises.*　　　**P. M**
[By Dr. WATTS.]

I'LL praise my Maker while I've breath;
　And when my voice is lost in death,
Praise shall employ my nobler powers;
My days of praise shall ne'er be past,
While life, and thought, and being last,
　Or immortality endures.

2 Happy the man whose hopes rely
On Israel's God; He made the sky,
　And earth, and seas, with all their train;

His truth forever stands secure ;
He saves th' oppress'd, He feeds the poor,
And none shall find His promise vain.

3 The Lord pours eyesight on the blind;
The Lord supports the fainting mind ;
He sends the lab'ring conscience peace ;
He helps the stranger in distress,
The widow and the fatherless,
And grants the pris'ner sweet release.

4 I'll praise Him while He lends me breath;
And when my voice is lost in death,
Praise shall employ my nobler powers ;
My days of praise shall ne'er be past,
While life, and thought, and being last,
Or immortality endures.

142 *Victory.* S. M.

[By CHARLES WESLEY.]

I THE good fight have fought, —
O when shall I declare!
The vict'ry by my Saviour got,
I long with Paul to share.

2 O may I triumph so,
When all my warfare 's past ;
And, dying, find my latest foe
Under my feet at last !

3 This blessed word be mine,
Just as the port is gain'd, —
Kept by the power of grace divine,
I have the faith maintain'd.

An' apostles of my Lord,
To whom it first was given,
They could not speak a greater word,
Nor all the saints in heaven.

143   *The Wandering Sheep.*   S. M.

[By Rev. Dr. BONAR, of Scotland.]

I WAS a wand'ring sheep,
  I did not love the fold;
I did not love my Shepherd's voice,
  I would not be controll'd;
I was a wayward child,
  I did not love my home;
I did not love my Father's voice,
  I loved afar to roam.

2 The Shepherd sought His sheep,
  The Father sought His child;
They follow'd me o'er vale and hill,
  O'er deserts, waste and wild;
They found me nigh to death
  Famish'd, and faint, and lone;
They bound me with the bands of love,
  They saved the wand'ring one.

3 Jesus my Shepherd is,
  'Twas He that loved my soul;
'Twas He that wash'd me in His blood,
  'Twas He that made me whole;
No more a wand'ring sheep,
  I love to be controll'd;
I love my tender Shepherd's voice,
  I love the peaceful fold.

144 *I would not live alway.* P. M.

[By WILLIAM AUGUSTUS MUHLENBERG, D. D., founder and rector of
St. Luke's Hospital, N. Y. This hymn first appeared in the *Episcopal
Recorder* in 1824. A Committee was appointed by the General Conven-
tion of the Protestant Episcopal Church to prepare a new hymn-book;
and this was offered by a member, and was at first rejected, Dr. Muhlenberg himself being a member of the Committee and voting against it. It
was subsequently adopted, and has been ever since immensely popular.]

I WOULD not live alway; I ask not to stay
Where storm after storm rises dark o'er
the way;
The few lurid mornings that dawn on us here
Are enough for life's joys, full enough for its
cheer.

2 I would not live alway; no — welcome the
tomb!
Since Jesus hath lain there, I dread not its
gloom:
There sweet be my rest till He bid me arise,
To hail Him in triumph descending the skies.

3 Who, who would live alway, away from his God,
Away from yon heaven, that blissful abode,
Where rivers of pleasure flow bright o'er the
plains,
And the noontide of glory eternally reigns?

4 There saints of all ages in harmony meet,
Their Saviour and brethren transported to
greet;
While anthems of rapture unceasingly roll,
And the smile of the Lord is the feast of the
soul.

145 *Rest for the Weary.* **P. M.**

I N the Christian's home in glory
  There remains a land of rest,
Where the Saviour's gone before me,
  To fulfill my soul's request.
There is rest for the weary, there is rest for
   the weary,
  There is rest for you.
On the other side of Jordan,
In the sweet fields of Eden,
Where the tree of life is blooming,
  There is rest for you.

2 He is fitting up my mansion,
  Which eternally shall stand;
My stay will not be transient
  In that holy, happy land.
  There is rest, etc.

3 Pain nor sickness e'er can enter;
  Grief nor woe my lot shall share;
But in that celestial centre
  I a crown of life shall wear.
  There is rest, etc.

4 Death itself shall then be vanished,
  And its sting shall be withdrawn;
Shout with gladness, O ye ransomed!
  Hail with joy the happy morn.
  There is rest, etc.

146   *Consecration.*   P. M.

[By Rev. HENRY FRANCIS LYTE, born in Scotland in 1793 ; died in 1847; and buried in Nice.]

PART I.

JESUS, I my cross have taken,
    All to leave and follow Thee,
Naked, poor, despised, forsaken —
    Thou, from hence, my all shalt be.
Perish every fond ambition —
    All I've sought, or hoped, or known ;
Yet how rich is my condition —
    God and heaven are all my own.

2 Let the world despise and leave me —
    They have left my Saviour too ;
Human hopes and looks deceive me,
    Thou art not like them untrue ;
And while Thou shalt smile upon me,
    God of wisdom, love, and might ;
Foes may hate, and friends may scorn me
    Show Thy face and all is bright.

3 Go, then, earthly fame and treasure —
    Come disaster, scorn, and pain ;
In Thy service, pain is pleasure ;
    With Thy favor loss is gain.
I have called Thee Abba, Father ;
    I have set my heart on Thee ;
Storms may howl, and clouds may gather :
    All must work for good to me.

PART II.

1 Man may trouble and distress me,
    'Twill but drive me to Thy breast ;

Life with trials hard may press me,
  Thou canst give me sweetest rest.
O, 'tis not in grief to harm me,
  While Thy love is left to me ;
O, 'twere not in joy to charm me,
  Were that joy unmixed with Thee !

2 Know, my soul, thy full salvation;
  Rise o'er sin and fear and care ;
Joy to find, in every station,
  Something still to do and bear.
Think what spirit dwells within thee,
  Think what Father's smiles are thine,
Think that Jesus died to win thee ;
  Child of heaven, canst thou repine ?

3 Haste thee on from grace to glory,
  Arm'd by faith, and wing'd by prayer ;
Heaven's eternal days before thee,
  God's own hand shall guide thee there
Soon shall close thine earthly mission,
  Soon shall pass thy pilgrim days :
Hope shall change to glad fruition —
  Faith to sight, and prayer to praise.

147   *Christ the Way.*   **L. M.**

[By Rev. JOHN CENNICK.]

JESUS, my All, to heaven is gone —
  He whom I fix my hopes upon ;
His track I see, and I'll pursue
The narrow way, till Him I view.

2 The way the holy prophets went,
The way that leads from banishment,

The King's high way of holiness,
I'll go, for all His paths are peace.

3 This is the way I long had sought,
And mourned because I found it not;
Till late I heard my Saviour say, ·
" Come hither, soul ; I am the way."

4 Lo ! glad I come ; and Thou, blest Lamb !
Wilt take me guilty as I am :
Nothing but sin I Thee can give ;
Nothing but love shall I receive.

5 Then will I tell to sinners round
How dear a Saviour I have found :
I'll point to Thy redeeming blood,
And say, " Behold the way to God."

148　　*The Reign of Christ..*　　**L. M.**

[By Dr. WATTS. Paraphrase of Psalm 72.]

JESUS shall reign where'er the sun
　　Does his successive journeys run ;
His kingdom spread from shore to shore,
Till moons shall wax and wane no more.

2 For Him shall endless prayer be made,
And endless praises crown His head ;
His name, like sweet perfume, shall rise
With every morning sacrifice.

3 People and realms, of every tongue,
Dwell on His love with sweetest song ;
And infant voices shall proclaim
Their early blessings on His name.

4 Blessings abound where'er He reigns ;
The prisoner leaps to loose His chains ;

The weary find eternal rest,
And all the sons of want are blest.

5 Let every creature rise and bring
Peculiar honors to our King,
Angels descend with songs again,
And earth repeat the loud Amen.

149   *The New Jerusalem.*   **C. M.**

[This hymn first became generally known by its appearance in a collection by James Montgomery, who declared that he was not the author, but that he considered it one of the finest in the language. There is a manuscript copy of about half the hymn now in the British Museum. It bears the initials "F. B. P." and the date "1616," and the words, "to the tune Diana." It is almost universally popular in Scotland. It is probably a descendant of an old Latin hymn.]

JERUSALEM! my happy home!
Name ever dear to me!
When shall my labors have an end,
In joy and peace, in thee?

2 O! when, thou city of my God,
Shall I thy courts ascend,
Where congregations ne'er break up,
Where Sabbaths have no end?

3 There happier bowers than Eden's bloom,
Nor sin nor sorrow know:
Blest seats! through rude and stormy scenes,
I onward press to you.

4 Why should I shrink at pain and woe?
Or feel at death dismay?
I've Canaan's goodly land in view,
And realms of endless day.

5 Jerusalem! my glorious home!
My soul still pants for thee:

Then shall my labors have an end
When I thy joys shall see.

150   *Joyfully.*   P. M.
[By Rev. W. II. HUNTER, an American Methodist clergyman.]

JOYFULLY, joyfully, onward I move,
Bound for the land of bright spirits above :
Angelic choristers sing as I come,
Joyfully, joyfully haste to thy home.

2 Soon with my pilgrimage ended below,
Home to that land of delight will I go ;
Pilgrim and stranger no more shall I roam,
Joyfully, joyfully resting at home.

3 Sounds of sweet melody fall on my ear :
Harps of the blessed, your voices I hear !
Rings with the harmony heaven's high dome,
Joyfully, joyfully haste to thy home.

4 Bright will the morn of eternity dawn,
Death shall be banish'd, His sceptre be gone :
Joyfully then shall I witness his doom,
Joyfully, joyfully, safely at home.

151   *" Joy to the World ! "*   C. M.
[By Dr. WATTS.]

JOY to the world ! the Lord is come !
Let earth receive her King ;
Let every heart prepare Him room,
And heaven and nature sing.

2 Joy to the world ! the Saviour reigns !
Let men their songs employ ;

9   123

While fields and floods, rocks, hills, and plains
    Repeat the sounding joy.

3 No more let sin and sorrow grow,
    Nor thorns infest the ground:
He comes to make His blessings flow
    Far as the curse is found.

4 He rules the world with truth and grace,
    And makes the nations prove
The glories of His righteousness,
    And wonders of His love.

152   *Comfort for Mourners.*   **L. M.**

By WILLIAM C. BRYANT. Rearranged and very slightly altered by the
Compilers.]

LET not the good man's trust depart,
    Though life its common gifts deny, —
Though with a pierced and broken heart,
    And spurn'd of men, he goes to die.

2 The light of smiles shall fill again
    The lids that overflow with tears;
And weary hours of woe and pain
    Are promises of happier years.

3 There is a day of sunny rest
    For every dark and troubled night;
Grief may abide an evening guest,
    Yet joy shall come with early light.

4 For God has mark'd each sorrowing **day,**
    And number'd every secret tear;
And heaven's eternal bliss shall pay
    For all His children suffer here.

153   *Lofty Joys.*   L. M.

[By Dr. WATTS.]

L ORD, how secure and blest are they
    Who feel the joys of pardon'd sin ;
Should storms of wrath shake earth and sea,
    Their minds have heaven and peace within.

2 The day glides sweetly o'er their heads,
    Made up of innocence and love;
And soft, and silent as the shades,
    Their nightly minutes gently move.

3 How oft they see th' heavenly hills,
    Where groves of living pleasure grow ;
And longing hopes, and cheerful smiles,
    Sit undisturb'd upon their brow.

4 They scorn to seek earth's golden toys,
    But spend the day, and share the night,
In numb'ring o'er the richer joys
    That heaven prepares for their delight.

154   *He Comes !*   P. M.

[By Rev. THOMAS OLIVERS, born in Wales 1725, and died in London 1799.
He was one of John Wesley's early assistants, who calls him his "noble
cobbler." This hymn was sung in St. Paul's Cathedral, London, in
1753, as an Advent hymn. " Such honor have " not "*all* His saints."
The hymn was suggested by Rev. i. 7.

L O! He comes in clouds descending,
    Once for favored sinners slain ;
Thousand thousand saints attending
    Swell the triumph of His train :
    Alleluia !
Christ appears on earth again.

2 Every eye shall now behold Him
    Robed in dreadful majesty;

125

They who set at naught and sold Him,
   Pierced and nailed Him to the tree,
      Deeply wailing,
   Shall the true Messiah see.

3 These dear tokens of His passion
   Still His dazzling body bears ;
Cause of endless exultation
   To His ransomed worshippers ;
      With what rapture
   Gaze we on those glorious scars.

4 Yea, amen, let all adore Thee,
   High on Thine eternal throne ;
Saviour, take the power and glory ;
   Claim the Kingdoms for Thine own ;
      O come quickly !
   Alleluia ! Amen.

155   *The Brink of Fate.*   **P. M.**

By CHARLES WESLEY. Suggested to him while standing upon Land's
   End, and seeing the ocean breaking at his feet.]

L O! on a narrow neck of land,
   'Twixt two unbounded seas, I stand,
      Secure, insensible :
   A point of time, a moment's space,
   Removes me to that heavenly place,
      Or shuts me up in hell.

2 O God, mine inmost soul convert,
   And deeply on my thoughtful heart
      Eternal things impress :
   Give me to feel their solemn weight,
   And tremble on the brink of fate,
      And wake to righteousness.

3 Before me place, in dread array,
The pomp of that tremendous day,
  When Thou with clouds shalt come
To judge the nations at Thy bar ;
And tell me, Lord, shall I be there
  To meet a joyful doom ?

4 Be this my one great business here —
With serious industry and fear
  Eternal bliss t' insure ;
Thine utmost counsel to fulfill,
And suffer all Thy righteous will,
  And to the end endure.

5 Then, Saviour, then my soul receive,
Transported from this vale, to live
  And reign with Thee above,
Where faith is sweetly lost in sight,
And hope in full, supreme delight,
  And everlasting love.

156   *Home.*   P. M.

[By Rev. DAVID DENHAM, an English Baptist minister.]

MID scenes of confusion and creature com-
      plaints,
How sweet to my soul is communion with saints :
To find at the banquet of mercy there 's room,
And feel, in the presence of Jesus, at home.
    Home, home, sweet, sweet home :
  Prepare me, dear Saviour, for heaven, my
      home.

2 Sweet bonds, that unite all the children of
    peace,
And thrice precious Jesus, whose love cannot
    cease :
Though oft from Thy presence in sadness I roam,
I long to behold Thee in glory, at home.

3 I sigh from this body of sin to be free,
Which hinders my joy and communion with Thee :
Though now my temptations like billows may
    foam,
All, all will be peace when I'm with Thee at
    home.

4 While here in the valley of conflict I stay,
O give me submission and strength as my day :
In all my afflictions to Thee would I come,
Rejoicing in hope of my glorious home. .

157   *Christmas Carol.*   C. M.

[By Rev. SAMUEL MEDLEY, an English Baptist clergyman. He had been
very profane in early life, and was converted under Whitefield's preaching. He was born 1738, and died in 1799.]

MORTALS, awake, with angels join,
    And chant the solemn lay ;
Joy, love, and gratitude combine,
    To hail th' auspicious day.

2 In heaven the rapt'rous song began,
    And sweet seraphic fire
Through all the shining legions ran ;
    And strung and tuned the lyre.

3 Swift through the vast expanse it flew,
    And loud the echo roll'd ;

The theme, the song, the joy, was new,—
'Twas more than heaven could hold.

4 Down through the portals of the sky
　The impetuous torrent ran ;
And angels flew, with eager joy,
　To bear the news to man.

5 With joy the chorus we repeat, —
　Glory to God on high !
Good-will and peace are now complete —
　Jesus was born to die.

6 Hail, Prince of life, forever hail !
　Redeemer, Brother, Friend !
Though earth, and time, and life shall fail,
　Thy praise shall never end.

158 　　*The Cross and the Crown.* 　　**C. M.**

[By G. N. ALLEN.]

MUST Jesus bear the cross alone,
　And all the world go free ?
No : there's a cross for every one,
　And there's a cross for me.

2 How happy are the saints above
　Who once went sorrowing here ;
But now they taste unmingled love,
　And joy without a tear.

3 The consecrated cross I'll bear,
　Till death shall set me free,
And then go home my crown to wear, —
　For there's a crown for me !

159   *The Shining Shore.*   **P. M.**

MY days are gliding swiftly by,
    And I, a pilgrim stranger,
Would not detain them as they fly, —
Those hours of toil and danger :
    For O ! we stand on Jordan's strand,
        Our friends are passing over ;
    And, just before, the shining shore
        We may almost discover.

2 We'll gird our loins, my brethren dear,
    Our distant home discerning,
Our absent Lord has left us word, —
    Let every lamp be burning :
        For O ! etc.

3 Should coming days be cold and dark,
    We need not cease our singing ;
That perfect rest nought can molest,
    Where golden harps are ringing :
        For O ! etc.

4 Let sorrow's rudest tempest blow,
    Each chord on earth to sever, —
Our King says " Come ; " and there's our home
    Forever and forever.
        For O ! etc.

160   *Courage, my Soul.*   **C. M.**

[By WILLIAM COWPER.]

MY span of life will soon be done,
    The passing moments say ;
As length'ning shadows o'er the mead
    Proclaim the close of day.

2 O that my heart might dwell aloof
   From all created things ;
And learn that wisdom from above
   Whence true contentment springs.

3 Courage, my soul ; thy bitter cross,
   In every trial here,
Shall bear thee to thy heaven above,
   But shall not enter there.

4 The sighing ones, that humbly seek
   In sorrowing paths below,
Shall in eternity rejoice,
   Where endless comforts flow.

5 Soon will the toilsome strife be o'er
   Of sublunary care,
And life's dull vanities no more
   This anxious breast ensnare.

6 Courage, my soul ; on God rely ;
   Deliv'rance soon will come ;
A thousand ways has Providence
   To bring believers home.

161   *The Gospel Banner.*   **P. M.**

[By THOMAS HASTINGS, Mus. Doc., born in Connecticut in 1784.]

NOW be the gospel banner
   In every land unfurl'd ;
And be the shout, Hosanna !
   Reëcho'd through the world :
Till every isle and nation,   -
   Till every tribe and tongue
Receive the great salvation,
   And join the happy throng.

2 What though th' embattled legions
 Of earth and hell combine ?
His arm, throughout their regions,
 Shall soon resplendent shine :
Ride on, O Lord, victorious !
 Immanuel, Prince of peace,
Thy triumph shall be glorious :
 Thine empire still increase.

3 Yes, Thou shalt reign forever,
 O Jesus, King of kings :
Thy light, Thy love, Thy favor,
 Each ransom'd captive sings :
The isles for Thee are waiting,
 The deserts learn Thy praise :
The hills and valleys greeting,
 The song responsive raise.

162 *Evening Worship.* **C. M.**

[By Rev. JOHN MASON, an English clergyman, who died in 1694.]

NOW from the altar of our hearts
 Let warmest thanks arise ;
Assist us, Lord, to offer up
 Our evening sacrifice.

2 This day God was our sun and shield,
 Our Keeper and our Guide ;
His care was on our weakness shown, —
 His mercies multiplied.

3 Minutes and mercies multiplied,
 Have made up all this day ;
Minutes came quick, but mercies **were**
 More swift and free than they.

4 New time, new favors, and new joys,
　Do a new song require :
　Till we shall praise Thee as we would,
　Accept our heart's desire.

163　　　　*The Stubborn Heart.*　　**L. M.**
　　　　　[By Rev. Joseph Hart.]

O FOR a glance of heavenly day
　　To take this stubborn heart away ;
And thaw, with beams of love divine,
This heart, this frozen heart of mine.

2 The rocks can rend ; the earth can quake
The seas can roar ; the mountains shake ;
Of feeling, all things show some sign,
But this unfeeling heart of mine.

3 To hear the sorrows Thou hast felt,
O Lord, an adamant would melt ;
But I can read each moving line,
And nothing moves this heart of mine.

4 Thy judgments too, which devils fear —
Amazing thought ! — unmoved I hear ;
Goodness and wrath in vain combine
To stir this stupid heart of mine.

5 But power divine can do the deed ;
And, Lord, that power I greatly need :
Thy Spirit can from dross refine,
And melt and change this heart of mine.

164　　　　*Praise His Power.*　　**C. M.**
　　　　　[By Charles Wesley.]

O FOR a thousand tongues, to sing
　　My great Redeemer's praise ;

The glories of my God and King,
The triumphs of His grace.

2 My gracious Master, and my God,
Assist me to proclaim,—
To spread, through all the earth abroad,
The honors of Thy Name.

3 Jesus!—the Name that charms our fears,
That bids our sorrows cease;
'Tis music in the sinner's ears,
'Tis life, and health, and peace.

4 He breaks the power of reigning sin,
He sets the pris'ner free;
His blood can make the foulest clean;
His blood avail'd for me.

5 He speaks,—and list'ning to His voice,
New life the dead receive;
The mournful, broken hearts rejoice;
The humble poor believe.

6 Hear Him, ye deaf; His praise, ye dumb,
Your loosen'd tongues employ;
Ye blind, behold your Saviour come;
And leap, ye lame, for joy.

165   *The Glorious Hope.*   **P. M.**
[By CHARLES WESLEY.]

O GLORIOUS hope of perfect love,
It lifts me up to things above;
It bears on eagles' wings;
It gives my ravish'd soul a taste,
And makes me for some moments feast
With Jesus' priests and kings.

2 Rejoicing now in earnest hope,
  I stand, and from the mountain top
    See all the land below :
  Rivers of milk and honey rise,   `
  And all the fruits of paradise
    In endless plenty grow.

3 A land of corn, and wine, and oil,
  Favor'd with God's peculiar smile,
    With every blessing blest ;
  There dwells the Lord our Righteousness,
  And keeps His own in perfect peace,
    And everlasting rest.

4 O that I might at once go up ;
  No more on this side Jordan stop,
    But now the land possess ;
  This moment end my legal years ;
  Sorrows and sins, and doubts and fears,
    A howling wilderness.

166   *Holy Vows.*   **L. M.**
           [By Dr. DODDRIDGE.]

O HAPPY day that fix'd my choice
    On Thee, my Saviour and my God !
  Well may this glowing heart rejoice,
    And tell its raptures all abroad.

2 'Tis done, the great transaction 's done ;
    I am my Lord's, and He is mine ;
  He drew me, and I follow'd on,
    Charm'd to confess the voice divine.

3 Now rest, my long-divided heart ;
    Fix'd on this blissful centre, rest ;

Nor ever from Thy Lord depart:
With Him of every good possess'd.

4 High Heaven, that heard the solemn vow,
That vow renew'd shall daily hear,
Till in life's latest hour I bow,
And bless in death a bond so dear.

167   *Joys of First Love.*   **P. M.**

[By CHARLES WESLEY.]

O HOW happy are they,
  Who the Saviour obey,
And have laid up their treasure above;
Tongue can never express
The sweet comfort and peace
Of a soul in its earliest love.

2 That sweet comfort was mine,
When the favor divine
I received through the blood of the Lamb
When my heart first believed,
What a joy I received, —
What a heaven in Jesus's name!

3 'Twas a heaven below
My Redeemer to know,
And the angels could do nothing more
Than to fall at His feet,   .
And the story repeat,
And the Lover of sinners adore.

4 Jesus all the day long
Was my joy and my song:
O that all His salvation might see;

He hath loved me, I cried,
He hath suffer'd and died,
To redeem even rebels like me.

5 O the rapturous height
Of that holy delight
Which I felt in the life-giving blood;
Of my Saviour possess'd,
I was perfectly blest,
As if fill'd with the fullness of God.

168   *Divine Love.*   P. M.

[By CHARLES WESLEY.]

O LOVE divine, how sweet thou art!
   When shall I find my willing heart
All taken up by Thee?
I thirst, I faint, I die to prove
The greatness of redeeming love, —
The love of Christ to me.

2 Stronger His love than death or hell;
Its riches are unsearchable;
The first-born sons of light
Desire in vain its depths to see;
They cannot reach the mystery,
The length, the breadth, the height.

3 God only knows the love of God:
O that it now were shed abroad
In this poor stony heart:
For love I sigh, for love I pine;
This only portion, Lord, be mine;
Be mine this better part.

4 O that I could forever sit
With Mary at the Master's feet!
Be this my happy choice:
My only care, delight, and bliss,
My joy, my heaven on earth, be this
To hear the Bridegroom's voice.

5 O that I could, with favor'd John,
Recline my weary head upon
The dear Redeemer's breast:
From care, and sin, and sorrow free,
Give me, O Lord, to find in Thee
My everlasting rest.

169 *Prayer for Help.* **L. M.**

[By CHARLES WESLEY.]

O THAT my load of sin were gone;
O that I could at last submit
At Jesus' feet to lay it down —
To lay my soul at Jesus' feet.

2 Rest for my soul I long to find:
Saviour of all, if mine Thou art,
Give me Thy meek and lowly mind,
And stamp Thine image on my heart.

3 Break off the yoke of inbred sin,
And fully set my spirit free;
I cannot rest till pure within, —
Till I am wholly lost in Thee.

4 Fain would I learn of Thee, my God;
Thy light and easy burden prove;
The cross all stain'd with hallow'd blood,
The labor of Thy dying love.

5 I would, but Thou must give the power;
   My heart from every sin release;
Bring near, bring near the joyful hour,
   And fill me with Thy perfect peace.

170   *Rapture.*   C. M.
           [By Dr. WATTS.]

O 'TIS delight without alloy,
     Jesus, to hear Thy name;
My spirit leaps with inward joy;
   I feel the sacred flame.

2 My passions hold a pleasing reign,
   When love inspires my breast, —
Love, the divinest of the train,
   The sov'reign of the rest.

3 This is the grace must live and sing,
   When faith and hope shall cease,
And sound from every joyful string
   Through all the realms of bliss.

4 Swift I ascend the heavenly place,
   And hasten to my home;
I leap to meet Thy kind embrace;
   I come, O Lord, I come.

5 Sink down, ye separating hills;
   Let sin and death remove;
'Tis love that drives my chariot wheels,
   And death must yield to love.

171   *Hallelujah.*   P. M.
           [By CHARLES WESLEY.]

O THOU God of my salvation,
     My Redeemer from all sin;

Moved by Thy divine compassion,
Who has died my heart to win,
I will praise Thee:
Where shall I Thy praise begin?

2 Though unseen, I love the Saviour;
He hath brought salvation near;
Manifests His pard'ning favor;
And when Jesus doth appear,
Soul and body
Shall His glorious image bear.

3 While the angel choirs are crying, —
Glory to the great I AM,
I with them will still be vying —
Glory! glory to the Lamb!
O how precious
Is the sound of Jesus' name!

4 Angels now are hov'ring round us,
Unperceived amid the throng;
Wond'ring at the love that crown'd us,
Glad to join the holy song:
Hallelujah,
Love and praise to Christ belong!

172   *Insatiate Love.*   **L. M.**

[From the Latin of St. BERNARD, who died 1153. While walking in the garden with his brother-monks, he would sometimes exclaim, " Dear brethren,
I must go; there is some One waiting for me in my cell." That One was
the object of his supreme love, whom he celebrates in this hymn.]

OF Him who did salvation bring,
I could forever think and sing;
Arise, ye needy, — He'll relieve;
Arise, ye guilty, — He'll forgive.

2 Ask but His grace, and lo, 'tis given ;
Ask, and He turns your hell to heaven :
Though sin and sorrow wound my soul,
Jesus, Thy balm will make it whole.

3 To shame our sins He blush'd in blood ;
He closed His eyes to show us God :
Let all the world fall down and know
That none but God such love can show.

4 'Tis Thee I love, for Thee alone
I shed my tears and make my moan ;
Where'er I am, where'er I move,
I meet the Object of my love.

5 Insatiate to this spring I fly ;
I drink, and yet am ever dry :
Ah ! who against Thy charms is proof?
Ah ! who that loves, can love enough ?

173 *The Promised Land.* C. M.

By SAMUEL STENNETT, D. D., an eminent English Baptist clergyman, a
personal friend of George III. " Stormy banks," as applied to Jordan, may
not be critically accurate, but the hymn just as it stands has become so
dear to many that we do not choose to touch a single word.]

ON Jordan's stormy banks I stand,
   And cast a wishful eye
To Canaan's fair and happy land,
   Where my possessions lie.

2 O the transporting, rapturous scene,
   ' That rises to my sight !
Sweet fields array'd in living green,
   And rivers of delight

3 There generous fruits that never fail,
   On trees immortal grow ;

There rock, and hill, and brook, and vale,
With milk and honey flow.

4 O'er all those wide-extended plains
Shines one eternal day;
There God the Son forever reigns,
And scatters night away.

5 No chilling winds, or pois'nous breath,
Can reach that healthful shore ;
Sickness and sorrow, pain and death,
Are felt and feared no more.

6 When shall I reach that happy place,
And be forever blest ?
When shall I see my Father's face,
And in His bosom rest ?

7 Fill'd with delight, my raptured soul
Would here no longer stay ;
Though Jordan's waves around me roll,
Fearless I'd launch away.

174   *One there is above all others.*   **P. M.**

[By Rev. JOHN NEWTON.]

ONE there is above all others
    Well deserves the name of Friend ;
His is love beyond a brother's,
    Costly, free, and knows no end :
They who once His kindness prove,
Find it everlasting love.

2 Which of all our friends to save us
    Could or would have shed their blood ?
But our Jesus died to have us
    Reconciled in Him to God :

This was boundless love indeed :
Jesus is a Friend in need.

3 Could we bear from one another
　　What He daily bears from us?
Yet this glorious Friend and Brother
　　Loves us though we treat Him thus:
Though for good we render ill,
He accounts us brethren still.

4 O! for grace our hearts to soften ;
　　Teach us, Lord, at length to love.
We, alas! forget too often
　　What a Friend we have above ;
But, when home our souls are brought,
We will love Thee as we ought.

175　　　　　*Redemption.*　　　　C. M.
[By Dr. WATTS.]

PLUNGED in a gulf of dark despair,
　　We wretched sinners lay,
Without one cheering beam of hope,
　　Or spark of glimm'ring day.

2 With pitying eyes the Prince of grace
　　Beheld our helpless grief ;
He saw, and O, amazing love !
　　He ran to our relief.

3 Down from the shining seats above
　　With joyful haste He fled,
Entered the grave in mortal flesh,
　　And dwelt among the dead.

4 He spoiled the powers of darkness thus,
　　And broke our iron chains ;

Jesus has freed our captive souls
From everlasting pains.

5 O for this love, let rocks and hills
Their lasting silence break,
And all harmonious human tongues
The Saviour's praises speak.

6 Angels, assist our mighty joys;
Strike all your harps of gold;
But when you raise your highest notes,
His love can ne'er be told.

176   *Prayer.*   L, M,
[By Rev. JOSEPH HART.]

PRAYER is appointed to convey
The blessings God designs to give:
Long as they live should Christians pray;
They learn to pray when first they live.

2 If pain afflict, or wrongs oppress;
If cares distract, or fears dismay;
If guilt deject; if sin distress;
In every case, still watch and pray.

3 'Tis prayer supports the soul that's weak:
Though thought be broken, language lame,
Pray, if thou canst or canst not speak;
But pray with faith in Jesus' name.

4 Depend on Him; thou canst not fail;
Make all thy wants and wishes known;
Fear not; His merits must prevail:
Ask but in faith, it shall be done.

177   *The Lord is King.*   P. M.

[By CHARLES WESLEY.]

REJOICE! the Lord is King;
   Your Lord and King adore;
Mortals, give thanks and sing,
   And triumph evermore!
Lift up your hearts, lift up your voice;
Rejoice! — again I say, rejoice!

2 Jesus, the Saviour, reigns,
   The God of truth and love;
When He had purged our stains,
   He took His seat above:
Lift up your hearts, lift up your voice;
Rejoice! — again I say, rejoice!

3 His kingdom cannot fail;
   He rules o'er earth and heaven;
The keys of death and hell
   Are to our Jesus given:
Lift up your hearts, lift up your voice;
Rejoice! — again I say, rejoice!

4 Rejoice in glorious hope:
   Jesus, the Judge, shall come,
And take His servants up
   To their eternal home:
We soon shall hear th' archangel's voice;
The trump of God shall sound, Rejoice!

178   *The Better Portion.*   P. M.

[By SEAGRAVE.]

RISE, my soul, and stretch thy wings;
   Thy better portion trace;

Rise from transitory things,
　Tow'rd heaven, thy native place:
Sun, and moon, and stars decay;
　Time shall soon this earth remove ·
Rise, my soul, and haste away
　To seats prepared above.

2 Rivers to the ocean run,
　Nor stay in all their course;
Fire, ascending, seeks the sun;
　Both speed them to their source:
So a soul that's born of God
　Pants to view His glorious face;
Upward tends to His abode,
　To rest in His embrace.

3 Cease, ye pilgrims, cease to mourn;
　Press onward to the prize;
Soon our Saviour will return
　Triumphant in the skies:
There we'll join the heavenly train,
　Welcomed to partake the bliss;
Fly from sorrow, care, and pain,
　To realms of endless peace.

179　　　*Evening Blessing.*　　　**P. M.**

[By JAMES EDMESTON, a Congregational layman, who died in London a
few years ago, at an advanced age.]

SAVIOUR, breathe an evening blessing,
　Ere repose our spirits seal:
Sin and want we come confessing;
　Thou canst save, and Thou canst heal.

2 Though destruction walk around us,
　Though the arrow near us fly,

Angel-guards from Thee surround us;
　We are safe, if Thou art nigh.

3 Though the night be dark and dreary,
　Darkness cannot hide from Thee:
Thou art He who, never weary,
　Watcheth where Thy people be.

4 Should swift death this night o'ertake us,
　And our couch become our tomb,
May the morn in heaven awake us,
　Clad in light and deathless bloom!

180　　*Condemned, but Pleading.*　　**L. M.**

[By Dr. WATTS. A paraphrase of the 51st Psalm.]

SHOW pity, Lord; O Lord, forgive;
　Let a repenting rebel live.
Are not Thy mercies large and free?
May not a sinner trust in Thee?

2 My crimes are great, but don't surpass
The power and glory of Thy grace;
Great God, Thy nature hath no bound, —
So let Thy pard'ning love be found.

3 O wash my soul from every sin,
And make my guilty conscience clean;
Here on my heart the burden lies,
And past offenses pain my eyes.

4 My lips with shame my sins confess,
Against Thy law, against Thy grace;
Lord, should Thy judgments grow severe,
I am condemn'd, but Thou art clear.

5 Yet save a trembling sinner, Lord,
Whose hope, still hov'ring round Thy word,

Would light on some sweet promise there, —
Some sure support against despair.

181   *God always Good.*   **C. M.**

[By Rev. JAMES HERVEY, author of "Meditations among the Tombs,"
born in 1714 ; died 1758.]

SINCE all the varying scenes of time
 God's watchful eye surveys,
O, who so wise to choose our lot,
 Or to appoint our ways!

2 Good, when He gives, supremely good ;
 Nor less when He denies :
Ev'n crosses, from His sovereign hand,
 Are blessings in disguise.

3 Why should we doubt a Father's love,
 So constant and so kind !
To His unerring, gracious will
 Be every wish resigned.

4 In Thy fair book of life divine,
 My God, inscribe my name ;
There let it fill some humble place
 Beneath my Lord the Lamb !

182   *Why will ye die?*   **P. M.**

[By CHARLES WESLEY.]

SINNERS, turn ; why will ye die ?
 God, your Maker, asks you why ?
God, who did your being give,
Made you with Himself to live ;
He the fatal cause demands ;
Asks the work of His own hands, —

Why, ye thankless creatures, why
Will ye cross His love, and die?

2 Sinners, turn; why will ye die?
God, your Saviour, asks you why?
He, who did your souls retrieve,
Died Himself, that ye might live.
Will ye let Him die in vain?
Crucify your Lord again?
Why, ye ransom'd sinners, why
Will ye slight His grace, and die?

3 Sinners, turn; why will ye die?
God, the Spirit, asks you why?
He, who all your lives hath strove,
Urged you to embrace His love.
Will ye not His grace receive?
Will ye still refuse to live?
O ye dying sinners, why,
Why will ye forever die?

183   *Stay, Spirit, stay!*   **L. M.**
[BY CHARLES WESLEY.]

STAY, thou insulted Spirit, stay!
  Though I have done Thee such despite,
Cast not a sinner quite away,
  Nor take Thine everlasting flight.

2 Though I have most unfaithful been
  Of all whoe'er Thy grace received;
Ten thousand times Thy goodness seen,
  Ten thousand times Thy goodness grieved;

3 Yet, O, the chief of sinners spare,
  In honor of my great High-Priest!

Nor, in Thy righteous anger, swear
I shall not see thy people's rest.
4 O Lord, my weary soul release,
    Upraise me by Thy gracious hand ,
Guide me into Thy perfect peace,
    And bring me to the promised land.

184   *Sweet Hour of Prayer.*   **L. M.**

SWEET hour of prayer, sweet hour of prayer,
    That calls me from a world of care,
And bids me at my Father's throne
Make all my wants and wishes known :
In seasons of distress and grief
My soul has often found relief,
And oft escaped the tempter's snare
By Thy return, sweet hour of prayer.
2 Sweet hour of prayer, sweet hour of prayer,
    May I thy consolations share,
Till from Mount Pisgah's lofty height
I view my home and take my flight :
This robe of flesh I'll drop, and rise
To seize the everlasting prize,
And shout, while passing through the air,
Farewell, farewell, sweet hour of prayer.

185   *The Spirit of Prayer.*   **S. M.**
        [By CHARLES WESLEY.]

THE praying spirit breathe !
    The watching power impart ;
From all entanglements beneath,
    Call off my peaceful heart ;

My feeble mind sustain,
  By worldly thoughts oppress'd;
Appear and bid me turn again
  To my eternal rest.

2 Swift to my rescue come;
  Thine own this moment seize;
Gather my wand'ring spirit home,
  And keep in perfect peace:
Suffer'd no more to rove
  O'er all the earth abroad,
Arrest the pris'ner of Thy love,
  And shut me up in God.

186 *The Fountain.* **C. M.**

[By WILLIAM COWPER.]

THERE is a fountain fill'd with blood,
  Drawn from Immanuel's veins;
And sinners, plunged beneath that flood,
  Lose all their guilty stains.

2 The dying thief rejoiced to see
  That fountain in his day;
And there may I, though vile as he,
  Wash all my sins away.

3 Thou dying Lamb! Thy precious blood
  Shall never lose its power,
Till all the ransom'd Church of God
  Are saved, to sin no more.

4 E'er since, by faith, I saw the stream
  Thy flowing wounds supply,
Redeeming love has been my theme,
  And shall be, till I die.

5 Then in a nobler, sweeter song,
  I'll sing Thy power to save,
When this poor lisping, stamm'ring tongue.
Lies silent in the grave.

187   *The Heavenly Canaan.*   **C. M.**

By Dr. WATTS. A learned English compiler rejects this hymn because of
the glaring defects of the last stanza, which have long been apparent to us,
which we think obviated by the slight alteration we have ventured to
make in the line next the last, which in the original is, "Not Jordan's
stream nor Death's cold flood." The criticism is that the stream and the
flood are the same or different. If different, what has the Jordan to do
with the departing soul? If the same, the line means "Not Jordan's
stream nor Jordan's stream," or "Not Death's cold flood nor Death's cold
flood," which is neither very clear nor very edifying.]

THERE is a land of pure delight,
  Where saints immortal reign ;
Infinite day excludes the night,
  And pleasures banish pain.

2 There everlasting spring abides,
  And never-with'ring flowers :
Death, like a narrow sea, divides
  This heavenly land from ours.

3 Sweet fields beyond the swelling flood
  Stand dress'd in living green ;
So to the Jews old Canaan stood,
  While Jordan roll'd between.

4 Could we but climb where Moses stood,
  And view the landscape o'er,
No Jordan stream of Death's cold flood
  Should fright us from the shore.

188   *The Sweetest Name.*   **P. M.**

THERE is no name so sweet on earth,
  No name so sweet in heaven,

The name, before His wondrous birth,
To Christ, the Saviour, given.

CHORUS.

We love to sing around our King,
And hail Him blessed Jesus;
For there's no word ear ever heard
So dear, so sweet as Jesus.

2 And when He hung upon the tree,
They wrote this name above Him,
That all might see the reason we
For evermore must love Him.

3 So now upon His Father's throne,
Almighty to release us
From sin and pains, He grandly reigns,
The Prince and Saviour Jesus.

189   *Immutable.*   **P. M.**

[By Rev. JOSEPH HART.]

THIS, this is the God we adore,
Our faithful, unchangeable Friend,
Whose love is as great as His power,
And neither knows measure nor end:
'Tis Jesus, the first and the last,
Whose Spirit shall guide us safe home;
We'll praise Him for all that is past,
And trust Him for all that's to come.

190   *The Lord will Provide.*   **P. M.**

[By Rev. JOHN NEWTON.]

THOUGH troubles assail, and dangers af-
fright,
Though friends should all fail, and foes all unite,

153

Yet one thing secures us, whatever betide,
The promise assures us, — The Lord will
provide.

2 The birds, without barn or storehouse, are fed ;
From them let us learn to trust for our bread :
His saints what is fitting shall ne'er be denied,
So long as 'tis written, — The Lord will pro-
vide.

3 No strength of our own, nor goodness we
claim :
Our trust is all thrown on Jesus's Name ;
In this our strong tower for safety we hide ;
The Lord is our power, — the Lord will pro-
vide.

4 When life sinks apace, and death is in view,
The word of His grace shall comfort us
through :
Not fearing or doubting, with Christ on our
side,
We hope to die shouting, — The Lord will
provide.

191   *Memorials of Grace.*   L. M.
          [By Dr. WATTS.]

THUS far the Lord hath led me on, —
    Thus far His power prolongs my days ;
And every evening shall make known
    Some fresh memorial of His grace.

2 Much of my time has run to waste,
    And I, perhaps, am near my home :

But He forgives my follies past,
   And gives me strength for days to come.

3 I lay my body down to sleep;
   Peace is the pillow for my head;
While well-appointed angels keep
   Their watchful stations round my bed.

4 Thus, when the night of death shall come,
   My flesh shall rest beneath the ground,
And wait Thy voice to rouse my tomb,
   With sweet salvation in the sound. .

192   *Dead and Alive.*   P. M.

[By ALICE CARY. Rearranged for this collection.]

TILL I learned to love Thy name,
   Lord, Thy grace denying,
I was lost in sin and shame,
   Dying, dying, dying!

2 Nothing could the world impart,
   Darkness held no morrow;
In my soul and in my heart,
   Sorrow, sorrow, sorrow!

3 When I learned to love Thy name,
   O Thou meek and lowly,
Rapture kindled to a flame, —
   Holy, holy, holy!

4 Henceforth shall creation ring
   With salvation's story,
Till I rise with Thee to sing,
   Glory, glory, glory!

193   *The Watchman.*   P. M.

[By JOHN BOWRING, LL. D.]

WATCHMAN, tell us of the night,
    What its signs of promise are.
Trav'ler, o'er yon mountain's height
    See the glory-beaming star.
Watchman, does its beauteous ray
    Aught of hope or joy foretell?
Trav'ler, yes, it brings the day —
    Promised day of Israel.

2 Watchman, tell us of the night;
    Higher yet that star ascends.
Trav'ler, blessedness and light,
    Peace and truth, its course portends.
Watchman, will its beams alone
    Gild the spot that gave them birth?
Trav'ler, ages are its own;
    See, it bursts o'er all the earth.

3 Watchman, tell us of the night,
    For the morning seems to dawn.
Trav'ler, darkness takes its flight;
    Doubt and terror are withdrawn.
Watchman, let thy wand'ring cease;
    Hie thee to thy quiet home.
Trav'ler, lo! the Prince of Peace,
    Lo! the Son of God is come.

194   *Blessings of Prayer.*   L. M.

[By WILLIAM COWPER.]

WHAT various hindrances we meet
    In coming to a mercy-seat;

Yet who that knows the worth of prayer,
But wishes to be often there ?

2 Prayer makes the darken'd cloud withdraw;
Prayer climbs the ladder Jacob saw;
Gives exercise to faith and love ;
Brings every blessing from above.

3 Restraining prayer, we cease to fight;
Prayer keeps the Christian's armor bright;
And Satan trembles when he sees
The weakest saint upon his knees.

195   *The Lovely Sonnet.*

WHEN for eternal worlds we steer,
  And seas are calm and skies are clear,
And faith in lively exercise,
And distant hills of Canaan rise,
The soul for joy then claps her wings,
And loud her lovely sonnet sings,
        Vain world, adieu !

2 With cheerful hope her eyes explore
Each landmark on the distant shore :
The trees of life, the pastures green,
The crystal stream — delightful scene !
Again for joy she claps her wings,
And loud her lovely sonnet sings,
        Vain world, adieu !

3 The nearer still she draws to land,
More eager all her powers expand;
With steady helm and free-bent sail,
Her anchor drops within the veil :

Again for joy she claps her wings,
And her celestial sonnet sings,
Glory to God!

196   *My Title.*   C. M.

[By Rev. Dr. WATTS. Andrew Jackson declared that he regarded the first
stanza of this hymn the best thing in English poetry.]

WHEN I can read my title clear
To mansions in the skies,
I bid farewell to every fear,
And wipe my weeping eyes.

2 Should earth against my soul engage,
And fiery darts be hurled,
Then I can smile at Satan's rage,
And face a frowning world.

3 Let cares like a wild deluge come,
And storms of sorrow fall;
May I but safely reach my home,
My God, my heaven, my all.

4 There shall I bathe my weary soul
In seas of heavenly rest,
And not a wave of trouble roll
Across my peaceful breast.

197   *Calvary.*   P. M

[By JAMES MONTGOMERY. Written in 1812.]

WHEN on Sinai's top I see
God descend. in majesty,
To proclaim His holy law,
All my spirit sinks with awe.

2 When, in ecstasy sublime,
Tabor's glorious steep I climb,
At the too transporting light,
Darkness rushes o'er my sight.

3 When on Calvary I rest,
God, in flesh made manifest,
Shines in my Redeemer's face,
Full of beauty, truth, and grace.

4 Here I would forever stay, —
Weep and gaze my soul away;
Thou art heaven on earth to me,
Lovely, mournful Calvary.

198   *Burial of Friends.*   C. M.
[By Dr. WATTS.]

WHY do we mourn departing friends,
Or shake at death's alarms?
'Tis but the voice that Jesus sends
To call them to His arms.

2 Are we not tending upward too
As fast as time can move?
Nor would we wish the hours more slow
To keep us from our love.

3 Where should the dying members rest,
But with their dying Head?
The graves of all the saints He blest,
And softened every bed;

4 Thence He arose, ascended high,
And showed our feet the way:
Up to the Lord our flesh shall fly,
At the great rising day.

199   *Gate of Joy.*   **L. M**
[By Dr. ISAAC WATTS.]

WHY should we start, and fear to die ?
　　What tim'rous worms we mortals are !
Death is the gate to endless joy,
　　And yet we dread to enter there.

2 The pains, the groans, the dying strife,
　　Fright our approaching souls away ;
And we shrink back again to life,
　　Fond of our prison and our clay.

3 O would my Lord His servant meet,
　　My soul would stretch her wings in haste,
Fly fearless through death's iron gate,
　　Nor feel the terrors as she pass'd.

4 Jesus can make a dying bed
　　Feel soft as downy pillows are,
While on His breast I lean my head,
　　And breathe my life out sweetly there.

200   *His Sympathy.*   **C. M.**
[By Dr. WATTS.]

WITH joy we meditate the grace
　　Of our High-Priest above ;
His heart is made of tenderness,
　　His bowels melt with love.

2 Touch'd with a sympathy within,
　　He knows our feeble frame ;
He knows what sore temptations mean,
　　For He hath felt the same.

3 He in the days of feeble flesh,
　　Pour'd out strong cries and tears,

And in His measure feels afresh
  What every member bears.

4 He'll never quench the smoking flax,
    But raise it to a flame ;
  The bruiséd reed He never breaks,
    Nor scorns the meanest name.

5 Then let our humble faith address
    His mercy and His power ;
  We shall obtain deliv'ring grace
    In every trying hour.

LYRICS.

201 *A mighty Fortress is our God.*

[Written by LUTHER, on his way to the Diet of Worms. In hours of despondency he was accustomed to say to Melancthon, " Come, Philip, let us sing the 46th Psalm." This version is by F. H. Hedge.]

A MIGHTY fortress is our God,
  A bulwark never failing ;
Our Helper He amid the flood
  Of mortal ills prevailing.·
    For still our ancient foe
    Doth seek to work us woe;
    His craft and power are great,
    And, armed with cruel hate,
  On earth is not his equal.

Did we in our own strength confide,
  Our striving would be losing ;
Were not the right Man on our side,
  The Man of God's own choosing.
    Dost ask who that may be ?
    Christ Jesus, it is He,
    Lord Sabaoth His name,
    From age to age the same,
  And He must win the battle.

And though this world, with devils fill'd,
  Should threaten to undo us,
We will not fear, for God hath willed
  His truth to triumph through us.

163

The Prince of Darkness grim,
  We tremble not for him ;
His rage we can endure,
For, lo ! his doom is sure,
  One little word shall fell him.
That word above all earthly powers —
  No thanks to them — abideth ;
The spirit and the gifts are ours
  Through Him who with us sideth.
  Let goods and kindred go,
  This mortal life also ;
The body they may kill,
God's truth abideth still,
  His kingdom is forever.

202   *The Stranger.*

Written in 1826, by JAMES MONTGOMERY, of England, son of a Moravian
minister ; born 1771 ; died 1854.]

A POOR wayfaring man of grief
  Hath often crossed me on my way,
Who sued so humbly for relief,
  That I could never answer, Nay.
I had not power to ask his name,
Whither he went, or whence he came,
Yet there was something in his eye
That won my love, I knew not why.

Once, when my scanty meal was spread,
  He entered, — not a word he spake, —
Just perishing for want of bread ;
  I gave him all ; he blessed it, brake,
And ate, — but gave me part again ;
Mine was an angel's portion then ;

For while I fed with eager haste,
That crust was manna to my taste.

I spied him, where a fountain burst
    Clear from the rock; his strength was gone;
The heedless water mocked his thirst,
    He heard it, saw it hurrying on:
I ran to raise the sufferer up;
Thrice from the stream he drained my cup,
Dipt, and returned it running o'er;
I drank and never thirsted more.

'Twas night; the floods were out; it blew
    A winter hurricane aloof;
I heard his voice abroad, and flew
    To bid him welcome to my roof;
I warmed, I clothed, I cheered my guest,
Laid him on my own couch to rest,
Then made the earth my bed, and seemed
In Eden's garden while I dreamed.

Stript, wounded, beaten nigh to death,
    I found him by the highway side;
I roused his pulse, brought back his breath,
    Revived his spirit, and supplied
Wine, oil, refreshment; he was healed:
I had myself a wound concealed;
But from that hour forgot the smart,
And peace bound up my broken heart.

In prison I saw him next, condemned
    To meet a traitor's death at morn;
The tide of lying tongues I stemmed,
    And honored him 'midst shame and scorn;

My friendship's utmost zeal to try,
He asked if I for him would die?
The flesh was weak, my blood ran chill,
But the free spirit cried, " I will."

Then in a moment to my view
    The stranger rose from his disguise ;
The tokens in his hands I knew ;
    My Saviour stood before mine eyes !
He spake, and my poor name He named :
" Of me thou hast not been ashamed ;
These deeds shall thy memorial be ;
Fear not, thou didst them unto me."

203   *Abide with Us.*

[By Rev. HENRY FRANCIS LYTE, born at Kelso, June, 1793 ; died at Nice
in 1847. This was his last hymn, written shortly before his death.]

ABIDE with me ; fast falls the eventide ;
    The darkness deepens ; Lord, with me
        abide :
When other helpers fail, and comforts flee,
Help of the helpless, O abide with me !

Swift to the close ebbs out life's little day ;
Earth's joys grow dim, its glories pass away ;
Change and decay in all around I see ;
O Thou who changest not, abide with me !

I need Thy presence every passing hour ;
What but Thy grace can foil the tempter's
        power?
Who, like Thyself, my guide and stay can be ?
Through cloud and sunshine, Lord, abide with
        me !

I fear no foe: with Thee at hand to bless,
Ills have no weight, and tears no bitterness;
Where is death's sting? where, grave, thy victory?
I triumph still, if Thou abide with me.

Hold Thou Thy cross before my closing eyes;
Shine through the gloom, and point me to the skies;
Heaven's morning breaks, and earth's vain shadows flee, —
In life, in death, O Lord, abide with me!

204.   *Sunday Evening.*

[By Mrs. CHARLES, author of Schönberg-Cotta Family. Written in 1867.]

ANOTHER day of heavenly rest
    And angels' toil is ended,
And to the chorus of the bless'd
    The last hymn has ascended.
Tranquil as an infant's sleep
    Night covers cot and meadow;
Let Thy peace with calm as deep
    The wearied spirit shadow.

As of old the apostle band
    All their labors bore Thee,
Lowly at Thy feet we stand,
    Lay our work before Thee.
Pardon Thou the imperfect deed,
    Crown the weak endeavor,
Prosper Thou the heavenly seed,
    Work Thou with us ever.

Let Thy Lambs we sought to feed
By Thy hand be nourish'd ;
Let them be Thy lambs indeed,
In Thy bosom cherish'd.
To the griefs we cannot reach
Breathe Thou consolation ;
To the hearts we cannot teach
Bring Thou Thy salvation.

205 . *The Heart's Prayer.*

[THOMAS MOORE, born in Dublin 1780; died 1852.]

A S, down in the sunless retreats of the ocean,
Sweet flowers are springing no mortal can
see,
So, deep in my soul, the still prayer of devotion,
Unheard by the world, rises, silent, to Thee,
My God ! silent, to Thee. —
Pure, warm, silent, to Thee.
As, still to the star of its worship, though
clouded,
The needle points faithfully o'er the dim sea,
So, dark when I roam, in this wintry world
shrouded,
The hope of my spirit turns, trembling, to
Thee,
My God ! trembling, to Thee, —
True, sure, trembling, to Thee.

206   *Stabat Mater.*

[Probably from the Latin of Jacobus de Benedictis, a Franciscan monk,
who died, 1306, at a great age; but the authorship is disputed. It is the
most pathetic, as the "Dies Iræ" is the grandest, of the Latin hymns. The
two concluding stanzas are from the "Mediæval Hymns" by Erastus C.
Benedict, published by Mr. Randolph. We do not know the translator
of the other stanzas, which came from "Hymns Ancient and Modern."]

A T the cross, her station keeping,
    Stood the mournful mother, weeping,
  Where He hung, her Son and Lord ;
For her soul of joy bereavéd,
Bowed with anguish deeply grievéd,
  Felt the sharp and piercing sword.

O how sad and sore distresséd —
Nor was she, that mother blessed
  Of the sole begotten One ;
Deep the woe of her affliction
When she saw the crucifixion
  Of her ever-glorious Son.

Who on Christ's dear mother gazing,
Pierced by anguish so amazing,
  Born of woman would not weep ?
Who on Christ's dear mother thinking,
Such a cup of sorrow drinking,
  Would not share her sorrows deep ?

For His people's sins chastiséd,
She beheld her Son despiséd,
  Scourged and crowned with thorny wreath ;
Saw Him then from judgment taken,
Mocked by foes, by friends forsaken,
  Till He gave His soul to death.

Jesus, may such deep devotion
Stir in me the same emotion,

Fount of love, Redeemer kind,
That my heart, fresh ardor gaining,
And a purer love attaining,
　May with Thee acceptance find.
All his stripes, O ! let me feel them ;
On my heart forever seal them,
　Printed there enduringly.
All His woes, beyond comparing,
For my sake in anguish bearing,
　Let me share them willingly.

On the Cross of Christ relying,
Through His death redeemed from dying,
　By His favor fortified ;
When my mortal frame is perished,
Let my spirit then be cherished,
　And in heaven be glorified.

207　　　*The Crucifixion.*

[By Rev. SAMUEL WESLEY, senior, father of John and Charles Wesley.
It was preserved from the fire which consumed the rectory at Epworth, in
1709, and copied from the scorched sheets.]

BEHOLD the Saviour of mankind
　Nail'd to the shameful tree ;
How vast the love that Him inclined
　To bleed and die for thee !

Hark ! how He groans, while nature shakes,
　And earth's strong pillars bend :
The temple's veil in sunder breaks, —
　The solid marbles rend.

'Tis done ! the precious ransom 's paid !
　Receive my soul ! He cries :

See where He bows His sacred head ;
He bows His head, and dies.
But soon He'll break death's envious chain,
And in full glory shine :
O Lamb of God, was ever pain,
· Was ever love, like Thine ?

208 *Bound upon the accursed Tree.*

[By HENRY HART MILMAN, D. D., Dean of St. Paul's, London, died in 1868.]

BOUND upon the accursed tree
Faint and bleeding, who is He ?
By the flesh with scourges torn,
By the crown of twisted thorn,
By the side so deeply pierced,
By the baffled burning thirst,
By the drooping death-dewed brow, —
Son of man, 'tis Thou ! 'tis Thou !

Bound upon the accursed tree,
Dread and awful, who is He ?
By the sun at noon-day pale,
Shiv'ring rock, and rending veil, —
Eden promised, ere he died,
To the felon at his side ;
Lord, our suppliant knees we bow, —
Son of God ! 'tis Thou ! 'tis Thou !

Bound upon the accursed tree,
Sad and dying, who is He !
By the last and bitter cry,
Ghost given up in agony,
By the lifeless body laid
In the chamber of the dead :

Crucified! we know Thce now, —
Son of man! 'tis Thou! 'tis Thou!
Bound upon the accursed tree,
Dread and awful, who is He?
By the spoiled and empty grave,
By the souls He died to save,
By the conquest He hath won,
By the saints before His throne,
By the rainbow round His brow, —
Son of God! 'tis Thou! 'tis Thou!

209   *" Brightest and Best."*

[By REGINALD HEBER, Bishop of Calcutta, born in England, 1783; died in 1827. This hymn written in 1826.]

BRIGHTEST and best of the sons of the
      morning,
Dawn on our darkness, and lend us thine aid;
Star of the East, the horizon adorning,
Guide where the infant Redeemer is laid.

Cold, on His cradle, the dew-drops are shining;
Low lies His bed with the beasts of the stall;
Angels adore Him, in slumber reclining, —
Maker, and Monarch, and Saviour of all.

Say, shall we yield Him, in costly devotion,
Odors of Eden, and off'rings divine?
Gems of the mountain, and pearls of the ocean,
Myrrh from the forest, and gold from the mine?

Vainly we offer each ample oblation;
Vainly with gifts would His favor secure;
Richer by far is the heart's adoration:
Dearer to God are the prayers of the poor.

210 *The Saint's Homesickness.*

We give in this lyric what we esteem the best stanzas in the Rev. J. M.
Neale's admirable version of the famous poem written in the twelfth century by Bernard of Clugny, beginning "Hic breve vivitur." Those who
have examined the original know that the poem contains nearly three
thousand lines, and is written in dactylic hexameters, uniting the leonine
and tailed rhyme. Every possible prosodial difficulty beset the author in
the task he assigned himself, and the popularity of the hymn is due to the
spirit of genuine poetry which has survived through the centuries in a
body so cramping and unpoetical.]

BRIEF life is here our portion,
   Brief sorrow, short-lived care ;
The life that knows no ending,
   The tearless life, is there.

And now we fight the battle,
   But then shall wear the crown
Of full and everlasting
   And passionless renown.

O one, O onely mansion !
   O Paradise of joy !
Where tears are ever banished,
   And smiles have no alloy.

Beside thy living waters
   All plants are, great and small ;
The cedar of the forest,
   The hyssop of the wall.

With jasper glow thy bulwarks ;
   Thy streets with emeralds blaze ;
The sardius and the topaz
   Unite in thee their rays.

Thy ageless walls are bonded
   With amethyst unpriced ;
Thy saints build up its fabric,
   And the corner stone is Christ.

Thou hast no shore, fair ocean !
  Thou hast no time, bright day !
Dear fountain of refreshment
  To pilgrims far away !
Upon the Rock of Ages
  They raise thy holy tower,
Thine is the victor's laurel,
  And thine the golden dower.

Thou feel'st in mystic rapture,
  O bride that know'st no guile,
The Prince's sweetest kisses,
  The Prince's loveliest smile.

Unfading lilies, bracelets
  Of living pearl, thine own ;
The Lamb is ever near thee,
  The Bridegroom thine alone.

Jerusalem the golden !
  With milk and honey blest,
Beneath thy contemplation
  Sink heart and voice opprest.

I know not, O, I know not
  What social joys are there,
What radiancy of glory,
  What light beyond compare ;
And when I fain would sing them,
  My spirit fails and faints,
And vainly would it image
  The assembly of the saints.

They stand, those halls of Syon,
  Conjubilant with song,

And bright with many an angel,
  And many a martyr throng:
There is the throne of David,
  And there, from toil released,
The shout of them that triumph,
  The song of them that feast;
And they, beneath their Leader,
  Who conquered in the fight,
Forever and forever
  Are clad in robes of white.
And there the band of prophets
  United praise ascribes,
And there the twelvefold chorus
  Of Israel's ransomed tribes:
The lily-beds of virgins,
  The roses' martyr-glow,
The cohort of the Fathers
  Who kept the faith below.

O fields that know no sorrow!
  O state that fears no strife!
O princely bowers! O land of flowers!
  O realm and home of life!

O sweet and blessed country,
  Shall I ever see thy face?
O sweet and blessed country,
  Shall I ever win thy grace?
I *have* the hope within me
  To comfort and to bless!
Shall I ever win the prize itself?
  O tell me, tell me, Yes!

Exult, O dust and ashes!
The Lord shall be thy part
His only, His forever,
Thou shalt be, and thou art!

211   *Longing for Heaven.*

BURST, ye emerald gates, and bring
      To my raptured vision,
All th' ecstatic joys that spring
      Round the bright elysian:
Lo! we lift our longing eyes,
Break, ye intervening skies,
Sun of righteousness, arise,
Ope the gates of paradise!

Floods of everlasting light
      Freely flash before Him:
Myriads, with supreme delight,
      Instantly adore Him:
Angel trumps resound His fame:
Lutes, of lucid gold, proclaim
All the music of His name:
Heaven echoing the theme.

Four-and-twenty elders rise
      From their princely station,
Shout His glorious victories,
      Sing His great salvation,
Cast their crowns before His throne,
Cry, in reverential tone,
Glory be to God alone,
Holy! holy! holy One!

Hark! the thrilling symphonies
  Seem, at once, to seize us:
Join we, too, the holy lays,
  Jesus, Jesus, Jesus!
Sweetest sound on mortal tongue,
Sweetest note in seraph's song,
Sweetest carol ever sung,
Shout we with the heavenly throng.

212   *Dust to Dust.*

[By Mrs. FELICIA HEMANS, born in Liverpool, Eng., Sept. 25, 1793; died May 16, 1835.]

CALM on the bosom of thy God,
  Fair spirit, rest thee now!
Ev'n while with us thy footsteps trod,
  His seal was on thy brow.

Dust, to its narrow house beneath!
  Soul, to its place on high!
They that have seen thy look in death
  No more may fear to die.

Lone are the paths, and sad the bowers,
  Whence thy meek smile is gone;
But O! a brighter home than ours,
  In heaven, is now thine own.

213   *Saturday Night.*

CHAFED and worn with worldly care,
  Sweetly, Lord, my heart prepare;
Bid the inward tempest cease;
Jesus, come, and whisper peace!
Hush the whirlwind of my will;
With Thyself my spirit fill;

End in calm this busy week —
Let the Sabbath gently break!
Sever, Lord, the earthly ties —
Fain my soul to Thee would rise;
Disentangle me from time —
Lift me to a purer clime;
Let me cast away my load —
Let me now draw nigh to God,
Gently, loving Jesus, speak —
End in calm this busy week.

Draw the curtain of repose,
While my weary eyelids close;
Steal my spirit while I rest —
Give me dreaming pure and blest;
Raise me with a cheerful heart —
Holy Ghost, Thyself impart;
Then the Sabbath day will be
Heaven brought down to earth and me.

214   *Watch, Pray, and Work!*

[By FREDRIKA BREMER, born in Finland in 1802.]

CHEEK grow pale, but heart be vigorous!
    Body fail, but soul have peace!
Welcome, pain! thou searcher rigorous!
    Slay me, but my faith increase.
Sin, o'er sense so softly stealing,
    Doubt, that would my strength impair,
Hence at once from life and feeling!
    Now my cross I gladly bear.
Up, my soul! with clear sedateness
    Read Heaven's law, writ bright and broad;

Up ♭ a sacrifice to greatness.
Truth, and goodness, — up to God !
Up to labor ! from thee shaking
Off the bonds of sloth, be brave !
Give thyself to prayer and waking ;
Toil some fainting heart to save !

215   *Veni Creator Spiritus.*

[The origin of this famous hymn is unknown. Its authorship has been attributed to Charlemagne, but on no sufficient grounds, so far as we can ascertain. In the revisal of its Liturgy in 1662, the Church of England retained it in its offices for ordaining priests and consecrating bishops. It was formerly used at the coronation of kings and emperors. The Roman Catholic Church still employs it at the creation of popes. It is one of the instances in which the English version surpasses the original.]

COME, Holy Ghost, our souls inspire
And lighten with celestial fire.
Thou the anointing Spirit art,
Who dost Thy sevenfold gifts impart.
Thy blessed unction from above   ·
Is comfort, life, and fire of love.
Enable with perpetual light
The dullness of our blinded sight.
Anoint and cheer our soiléd face
With the abundance of Thy grace.
Keep far our foes, give peace at home :
Where Thou art Guide, no ill can come.
Teach us to know the Father, Son,
And Thee of both to be but One ;
That through the ages all along,
This may be our endless song :
Praise to Thine eternal merit,
Father, Son, and Holy Spirit.

216 " *The whole Family in Heaven and Earth.*"

[By Rev. CHARLES WESLEY. Some years after his death, his brother John was officiating in City Road Chapel, London. After prayer, while the people were expecting the hymn, he stood silent for a long space, with his eyes closed. At length he solemnly repeated this hymn written by his deceased brother. The effect upon those who knew both these saintly men, is said to have been overwhelming.]

COME, let us join our friends above,
   That have obtained the prize ;
And on the eagle wings of love
   To joys celestial rise.

Let all the saints terrestrial sing,
   With those to glory gone ;
For all the servants of our King,
   In earth and heaven, are one.

One family we dwell in Him,
   One church above, beneath,
Though now divided by the stream,
   The narrow stream, of death.

One army of the living God,
   To His command we bow ;
Part of His host have crossed the flood,
   And part are crossing now.

Ten thousand to their endless home
   This solemn moment fly ;
And we are to the margin come,
   And we expect to die.

O that we now might grasp our Guide !
   O that the word were given !
Come, Lord of Hosts, the waves divide,
   And land us all in heaven.

217   *"Come, let us Pray."*

COME, let us pray : 'tis sweet to feel
     That God Himself is near ;
That, while we at His footstool kneel,
     His mercy deigns to hear :
Though sorrows cloud life's dreary way,
This is our solace, — let us pray.

Come, let us pray : the burning brow,
     The heart oppressed with care,
And all the woes that throng us now,
     Will be relieved by prayer :
Our God will chase our griefs away ;
O glorious thought ! — come, let us pray.

Come, let us pray : the mercy-seat
     Invites the fervent prayer ;
Our Heavenly Father waits to greet
     The contrite spirit there :
O loiter not, nor longer stay
From Him who loves us ; — let us pray.

218   *"Prepare ye the Way of the Lord."*

[BY CHARLES WESLEY.]

COMFORT, ye ministers of grace,
     Comfort the people of your Lord ;
O lift ye up the fallen race,
     And cheer them by the Gospel word.
Go into every nation, go ;
     Speak to their trembling hearts, and cry,--
Glad tidings unto all we show :
     Jerusalem, thy God is nigh.

Hark! in the wilderness a cry,
　A voice that loudly calls, — Prepare;
Prepare your hearts, for God is nigh,
　And waits to make His entrance there.

The Lord your God shall quickly come;
　Sinners, repent, the call obey:
Open your hearts to make him room;
　Ye desert souls, prepare the way.

The Lord shall clear His way through all;
　Whate'er obstructs, obstructs in vain;
The vale shall rise, the mountain fall,
　Crooked be straight, and rugged plain.

The glory of the Lord display'd
　Shall all mankind together view;
And what His mouth in truth hath said,
　His own almighty hand shall do.

219 *Dies Iræ.*

[Written by THOMAS OF CELANO, a monk of the order of the Minorites.
He died in 1253, and this poem was found after his death, in a box
that belonged to him.　There are seventy English translations extant.
Crashaw's is the earliest.　Its introduction into Faust, by Gœthe, has
given it increased popularity in modern literature.　Dr. Samuel Johnson
could never repeat the tenth stanza in the original without tears.　Sir Walter Scott was frequently heard murmuring passages of it in his last ill-
ness.　Lord Roscommon died, it is said, repeating with great devotion two
lines of his own translation, —

　　"My God, my Father, and my Friend,
　　　Do not forsake me in my end."

　We have found the version by Hon. John A. Dix to combine, in the
whole, more literalness and poetry than any other entire translation.
That by Dr. S. J. Irons is regarded as the best in England.　We have
combined these two, giving in brackets the stanzas by Irons; the others
are by Dix, except the first, which is by another hand.]

DAY of wrath! that day of burning,
　　Earth and heaven to ashes turning,
Saint and Sibyl were discerning.

Ah ! what terror is impending,
When the Judge is seen descending,
And each secret veil is rending.

[Wondrous sound the trumpet flingeth,
Through earth's sepulchres it ringeth,
All before the throne it bringeth !]

Death and Nature, mazed, are quaking,
When, the grave's long slumber breaking,
Man to judgment is awaking.

[Lo ! the book exactly worded.
Wherein all hath been recorded ! —
Thence shall judgment be awarded.]

[When the Judge His seat attaineth, .
And each hidden deed arraigneth,
Nothing unavenged remaineth.]

What shall I then say, unfriended,
By no advocate attended,
When the just are scarce defended?

[King of Majesty tremendous,
Who dost free salvation send us,
Fount of Pity ! then befriend us.]

Holy Jesus, meek, forbearing,
For my sins the death-crown wearing,
Save me, in that day, despairing.

Worn and weary Thou hast sought me ;
By Thy cross and passion bought me ; —
[Shall such grace be vainly brought me?]

Righteous Judge of retribution,
Give, O give me absolution
Ere the day of dissolution.

[Guilty, now, I pour my moaning,
All my shame with anguish owning!
Spare, O God, Thy suppliant groaning!]

Thou to Mary gav'st remission,
Heard'st the dying thief's petition,
Bad'st me hope in my contrition.

In my prayers no grace discerning,
Yet on me Thy favor turning,
Save my soul from endless burning!

Give me, when Thy sheep confiding
Thou art from the goats dividing,
On Thy right a place abiding!

When the wicked are confounded,
And by bitter flames surrounded,
Be my joyful pardon sounded!

[Low I kneel, with heart submission —
See, like ashes, my contrition —
Help me in my last condition!]

Day of weeping, when from ashes
Man shall rise 'mid lightning flashes,
Guilty, trembling with contrition,
Save him, Father, from perdition!

220   *Days of my Youth.*

[By St. GEORGE TUCKER, an accomplished scholar, Judge of the United
States District Court for Eastern Virginia, born 1752 ; died 1827.]

DAYS of my youth, ye have glided away:
    Hairs of my youth, ye are frosted and
        gray:
Eyes of my youth, your keen sight is no more
Cheeks of my youth, ye are furrow'd all o'er:

Strength of my youth, all your vigor is gone :
Thoughts of my youth, your gay visions are
    flown.

Days of my youth, I wish not your recall :
Hairs of my youth, I'm content ye should fall :
Eyes of my youth, you much evil have seen :
Cheeks of my youth, bathed in tears you have
    been :
Thoughts of my youth, you have led me astray :
Strength of my youth, why lament your decay ?

Days of my age, ye will shortly be past :
Pains of my age, yet a while you can last :
Joys of my age, in true wisdom delight :
Eyes of my age, be religion your light :
Thoughts of my age, dread ye not the cold sod :
Hopes of my age, be fix'd on your God.

221 *The Miracle.*

'By Rev. JAMES FREEMAN CLARKE, born in New Hanover, New Hampshire, in 1802, now resides in Boston. This poem was written in 1856.]

DEAR Friend, whose presence in the house,
    Whose gracious word benign,
Could once at Cana's wedding feast
    Turn water into wine, —

Come visit us, and when dull work
    Grows weary, line on line,
Revive our souls, and make us see
    Life's water glow as wine.

Gay mirth shall deepen into joy,
    Earth's hopes shall grow divine,
When Jesus visits us, to turn
    Life's water into wine.

The social talk, the evening fire
　　The homely household shrine,
Shall glow with angels' visits when
　　The Lord pours out the wine!

For when self-seeking turns to love, .
　　Which knows not mine and thine,
The miracle again is wrought,
　　And water changed to wine.

222　　　*Nothing Fair on Earth.*

[By ANGELUS SILESIUS, born 1624; died 1677.　This version is by Frances
Elizabeth Cox, 1841.]

EARTH has nothing sweet or fair,
　　Lovely forms or beauties rare,
But before my eyes they bring
Christ, of beauty Source and Spring.

When the morning paints the skies,
When the golden sunbeams rise,
Then my Saviour's form I find
Brightly imaged on my mind.

When the day-beams pierce the night,
Oft I think on Jesus' light,
Think how bright that light will be,
Shining through eternity.

When, as moonlight softly steals,
Heaven its thousand eyes reveals,
Then I think : who made their light
Is a thousand times more bright.

When I see, in spring-tide gay,
Fields their varied tints display,

Wakes the thrilling thought in me,
What must their Creator be!

Sweetness fills the air around,
At the echo's answering sound;
But more sweet than echo's fall,
Is to me the Bridegroom's call.

Come, Lord Jesus! and dispel
This dark cloud in which I dwell;
Thus to me the power impart,
To behold Thee as Thou art.

223   *Thy will, not Mine.*

[By ANNA L. WARING.]

FATHER, I know that all my life
   Is portioned out for me;
The changes that will surely come
   I do not fear to see;
I ask Thee for a present mind,
   Intent on pleasing Thee.

I ask Thee for a thoughtful love,
   Through constant watching wise,
To meet the glad with joyful smiles,
   And wipe the weeping eyes;
A heart at leisure from itself,
   To soothe and sympathize.

I would not have the restless will
   That hurries to and fro,
That seeks for some great thing to do,
   Or secret thing to know:
I would be treated as a child,
   And guided where I go.

Wherever in the world I am,
 In whatsoe'er estate,
I have a fellowship with hearts,
 To keep and cultivate;
A work of lowly love to do
 For Him on whom I wait.

I ask Thee for the daily strength,
 To none that ask denied,
A mind to blend with outward life,
 While keeping at Thy side;
Content to fill a little space,
 If Thou be glorified.

And if some things I do not ask,
 Among my blessings be,
I'd have my spirit filled the more
 With grateful love to Thee;
More careful — not to serve Thee much,
 But please Thee perfectly.

224   *The Universal Prayer.*

[By ALEXANDER POPE.]

FATHER of all! in every age,
 In every clime adored,
By saint, by savage, or by sage,
 Jehovah, Jove, or Lord!

Thou great First Cause! least understood,
 Who all my sense confined,
To know but this, — that Thou art good,
 And that myself am blind;

Yet gave me in this dark estate,
 To see the good from ill;

And binding nature fast in fate,
Left free the human will ;

What conscience dictates to be done,
Or warns me not to do,
This teach me, more than hell, to shun,
That more than heaven pursue.

If I am right, Thy grace impart
Still in the right to stay ;
If I am wrong, O teach my heart
To find that better way.

Save me alike from foolish pride
Or impious discontent,
At aught Thy wisdom has denied,
Or aught Thy goodness lent.

Teach me to feel another's woe,
To hide the fault I see ;
The mercy I to others show,
That mercy show to me.

This day be bread and peace my lot,
All else beneath the sun
Thou knowest if best bestowed or not,
And let Thy will be done.

225 *Battle-Song.*

By ALTENBERG, 1631, and sung by the Evangelical army at the battle of
Leipsic, Sept. 7, 1631. It became the battle-song of Gustavus Adolphus.
He sang it for the last time, on entering the field of Lützen against Wallen
stein, his last victory, the field of his triumphant death.]

FEAR not, O little flock, the foe
Who madly seeks your overthrow ;
Dread not his rage and power :

What though your courage sometimes faints!
This seeming triumph o'er God's saints
   Lasts but a little hour.

Fear not! be strong! your cause belongs
To Him who can avenge your wrongs;
   Leave all to Him, our Lord:
Though hidden yet from all our eyes,
He sees His Gideon who shall rise!
   He girdeth on his sword!

As sure as God's own promise stands,
Not earth, nor hell, with all their bands,
   Against us shall prevail:
The Lord shall mock them from His throne;
God is with us, we are His own;
   Our vict'ry cannot fail!

Amen! Lord Jesus, grant our prayer;
Great Captain! now Thine arm make bare;
   Fight for us once again:
So shall all saints and martyrs raise
A joyful chorus to thy praise,
   World without end.   Amen.

226   *" Friend after Friend departs."*

[By JAMES MONTGOMERY, 1824.]

FRIEND after friend departs:
   Who hath not lost a friend?
There is no union here of hearts
   That finds not here an end:
Were this frail world our only rest,
Living or dying, none were blest.

Beyond the flight of time,
    Beyond this vale of death,
There surely is some blessed clime
    Where life is not a breath,
Nor life's affection transient fire,
Whose sparks fly upward to expire.

    There is a world above,
        Where parting is unknown;
A whole eternity of love,
        Form'd for the good alone:
And faith beholds the dying here
Translated to that happier sphere.

    Thus star by star declines,
        Till all are pass'd away,
As morning high and higher shines,
        To pure and perfect day;
Nor sink those stars in empty night, —
They hide themselves in heaven's own light.

227   *With the Lord.*

[By JAMES MONTGOMERY.]

FOREVER with the Lord!
    Amen, so let it be!
Life from the dead is in that word,
    'Tis immortality.

Here in the body pent,
    Absent from Him I roam;
Yet nightly pitch my moving tent
    A day's march nearer home.

Forever with the Lord!
    Father, if 'tis Thy will,

The promise of that faithful word,
E'en *here* to me fulfill.

So when my latest breath
Shall rend the veil in twain,
By death I shall escape from death,
And life eternal gain.

Knowing as I am known,
How shall I love that word,
And oft repeat before the throne,
Forever with the Lord!

228   *Light shining out of Darkness.*

[By WILLIAM COWPER, born 1731; died 1800. He was subject to fits of profound melancholy, sometimes amounting to mental derangement. In one of these he went from Olney, where he resided, to drown himself in a particular part of the River Ouse. He hired a chaise and driver who knew the way, having frequently visited the spot. On this occasion he unaccountably lost his way, and several hours were vainly consumed in striving to find it. Thus the spell was broken, and Cowper returned to his study to write this hymn, which has been so wonderfully instructive and comforting to thousands. The title above is that assigned by Cowper. This hymn is the last he ever composed for the Olney collection.]

GOD moves in a mysterious way,
His wonders to perform ;
He plants His footsteps in the sea,
And rides upon the storm.

Deep in unfathomable mines
Of never failing skill,
He treasures up His bright designs,
And works His sov'reign will.

Ye fearful saints, fresh courage take :
The clouds ye so much dread
Are big with mercy, and shall break
In blessings on your head.

Judge not the Lord by feeble sense,
  But trust Him for His grace ;
Behind a frowning providence
  He hides a smiling face.

His purposes will ripen fast,
  Unfolding every hour :
The bud may have a bitter taste,
  But sweet will be the flower.

Blind unbelief is sure to err,
  And scan His work in vain :
God is His own interpreter,
  And He will make it plain.

229   *Charity.*

[By Dr. Isaac Watts.   A paraphrase of 1 Cor. xiii. 1-3.]

HAD I the tongues of Greeks and Jews,
  And nobler speech than angels use,
If love be absent, I am found
Like tinkling brass, an empty sound.

Were I inspired to preach and tell
All that is done in heaven and hell,
Or could my faith the world remove,
Still I am nothing without love.

Should I distribute all my store
To feed the bowels of the poor,
Or give my body to the flame
To gain a martyr's glorious name :

If love to God and love to men
Be absent, all my hopes are vain :
Nor tongues, nor gifts, nor fiery zeal,
The works of love can e'er fulfill.

230   *Wisdom.*

[By CHARLES WESLEY.   A paraphrase of Proverbs iii. 13-18.]

HAPPY the man that finds the grace,
The blessing of God's chosen race,
The wisdom coming from above,
The faith that sweetly works by love.

Happy, beyond description, he
Who knows "the Saviour died for me!"
The gift unspeakable obtains,
And heavenly understanding gains.

Wisdom divine! who tells the price
Of wisdom's costly merchandise?
Wisdom to silver we prefer,
And gold is dross compared with her.

Her hands are fill'd with length of days,
True riches and immortal praise —
Riches of Christ on all bestow'd,
And honor that descends from God.

To purest joys she all invites,
Chaste, holy, spiritual delights:
Her ways are ways of pleasantness,
And all her flowery paths are peace.

Happy the man who wisdom gains:
Thrice happy who his guest retains:
He owns, and shall forever own,
Wisdom, and Christ, and heaven are one.

231 *Step by Step.*

HEAVEN is not reached by a single bound;
But we build the ladder by which we
rise
From the lowly earth to the vaulted skies,
And we mount to its summit round by round.

I count these things to be grandly true,
That a noble deed is a step toward God —
Lifting the soul from the common sod
To a purer air and a broader view.

We rise by the things that are under our feet,
By what we have mastered in greed and
gain,
By the pride deposed and the passion slain,
And the vanquished ill we hourly meet.

We hope, we resolve, we aspire, we trust,
When the morning calls to life and light;
But our hearts grow weary, and ere the night
Our lives are trailing in the sordid dust.

Wings for the angels, but feet for the men;
We must borrow the wings to find the way—
We may hope and resolve, and aspire and
pray,
But our feet must rise or we fall again.

Only in dreams is the ladder thrown
From the weary earth to the sapphire wall;
But the dreams depart, and the visions fall,
And the sleeper wakes on his pillow of stone.

Heaven is not reached at a single bound;
But we build the ladder by which we rise
From the lowly earth to the vaulted skies,
And we mount to its summit round by round.

232   *Adeste, fideles.*

[In the measure of the original.]

HITHER, ye faithful, adoring triumphant,
Come, come, and your off'ring to Beth-
lehem bring;
Lo! He is born who is Monarch of angels:
O come, let us worship the sovereign King.

He is the God of God, Light of Light, own
him,
Though He from the womb of the Virgin
doth spring;
He is the true God, not made but begotten:
O come, let us worship the sovereign King.

Now the glad chorus of angels is singing,
O how the great palace celestial doth ring!
Let there be glory to God in the highest:
O come, let us worship the sovereign King

Jesus, because of Thy birth we extol Thee,
This day shall Thy people their offerings
bring:
Word of the Father, eternal, incarnate:
O come, let us worship the sovereign King.

233   *Veni Sancte Spiritus.*

[Written by ROBERT, son of Hugh Capet, whom he succeeded on the throne
of France, A. D. 9.)7. He was a lovely soul, whose gentleness unfitted him
to be a monarch in rude and stormy times. He will be known for ages
through his hymn of Veni Sancte Spiritus.]

HOLY Spirit, come, we pray,
   Come from heaven and shed the ray
     Of Thy light divine.
Come, Thou Father of the poor,
Giver from a boundless store,
     Light of hearts, O shine !
Matchless Comforter in woe,
Sweetest Guest the soul can know,
     Living waters blest.
When we weep, our solace sweet,
Coolest shade in summer heat,
     In our labor rest.
Holy and most blessed light,
Make our inmost spirits bright
     With Thy radiance mild ;
For without Thy sacred powers,
Nothing can we own of ours,
     Nothing undefiled.
What is arid, fresh bedew ;
What is sordid, cleanse anew ;
     Balm on the wounded pour
What is rigid, gently bend ;
On what is cold, Thy fervor send ;
     What has stray'd, restore.
To Thine own in every place
Give the sacred sevenfold grace,
     Give Thy faithful this.

Give to virtue its reward,
Safe and peaceful end afford,
Give eternal bliss.

234   *Traveller's Hymn.*

Written in 1700 by Joseph Addison, upon his return from a tour on the
Continent.]

HOW are Thy servants blest, O Lord!
How sure is their defense !
Eternal wisdom is their guide,
Their help, omnipotence.

In foreign realms and lands remote,
Supported by Thy care,
Through burning climes they pass unhurt,
And breathe in tainted air.

When by the dreadful tempest borne
High on the broken wave,
They know Thou art not slow to hear,
Nor impotent to save.

The storm is laid, the winds retire,
Obedient to Thy will;
The sea, that roars at Thy command,
At Thy command is still.

In midst of dangers, fears, and deaths,
Thy goodness I'll adore ;
I'll praise Thee for Thy mercies past,
And humbly hope for more.

My life, while Thou preserv'st that life,
Thy sacrifice shall be ;
And death, when death shall be my lot,
Shall join my soul to Thee.

235   *Death of the Righteous.*

[By Mrs. BARBAULD.]

HOW blest the righteous when he dies!
    When sinks a weary soul to rest!
How mildly beam the closing eyes!
How gently heaves th' expiring breast!

So fades a summer cloud away;
    So sinks the gale when storms are o'er;
So gently shuts the eye of day;
So dies a wave along the shore.

A holy quiet reigns around, —
    A calm which life nor death destroys:
And naught disturbs that peace profound
Which his unfetter'd soul enjoys.

Life's labor done, as sinks the clay,
    Light from its load the spirit flies,
While heaven and earth combine to say, —
How blest the righteous when he dies!

236   *Zion's Watchmen.*

[By Dr. ISAAC WATTS. Paraphrase of Isaiah lii. 7.]

HOW beauteous are their feet
    Who stand on Zion's hill, —
Who bring salvation on their tongues,
    And words of peace reveal!

How charming is their voice, —
    So sweet the tidings are;
Zion, behold thy Saviour King;
    He reigns and triumphs here.

How happy are our ears,
   That hear the joyful sound,
Which kings and prophets waited for,
   And sought, but never found.

How blessed are our eyes,
   That see this heavenly light;
Prophets and kings desired it long,
   But died without the sight.

The watchmen join their voice,
   And tuneful notes employ;
Jerusalem breaks forth in songs,
   And deserts learn the joy.

The Lord makes bare His arm
   Through all the earth abroad:
Let every nation now behold
   Their Saviour and their God.

237   *The Eternal Years.*

[By Frederick Faber.]

HOW shalt thou bear the cross that now
   So dread a weight appears?
Keep quietly to God, and think
   Upon the Eternal Years.

Brave quiet is the thing for thee,
   Chiding thy scrupulous fears;
Learn to be real from the thought
   Of the Eternal Years.

One cross can sanctify a soul;
   Late saints and ancient seers
Were what they were because they mused
   Upon the Eternal Years.

Death will have rainbows round it seen
Through calm contrition's tears,
If tranquil Hope but trims her lamp
At the Eternal Years.

238 *The Evening.*

[By Mrs. PHŒBE H. BROWN, the faithful mother of many children, one of whom is now a missionary in the East. Mothers may take an interest in knowing that in the original the second line reads, " From children and from care."]

I LOVE to steal awhile away
From every cumb'ring care,
And spend the hours of setting day
In humble, grateful prayer.

I love in solitude to shed
The penitential tear,
And all His promises to plead
Where none but God can hear.

I love to think on mercies past,
And future good implore, —
And all my cares and sorrows cast
On Him whom I adore.

I love by faith to take a view
Of brighter scenes in heaven ;
The prospect doth my strength renew,
While here by tempests driven.

Thus, when life's toilsome day is o'er
May its departing ray
Be calm as this impressive hour,
And lead to endless day.

239   *My Psalm.*

[By John Greenleaf Whittier, born in Haverhill, Mass., 1808.]

I MOURN no more my vanished years:
　　Beneath a tender rain,
An April rain of smiles and tears,
　　My heart is young again.

The west winds blow, and, singing low,
　　I hear the glad streams run;
The windows of my soul I throw
　　Wide open to the sun.

No longer forward nor behind
　　I look in hope or fear;
But, grateful, take the good I find,
　　The best of now and here.

I plough no more a desert land,
　　To harvest weed and tare;
The manna dropping from God's hand
　　Rebukes my painful care.

I break my pilgrim staff — I lay   .
　　Aside my toiling oar;
The angel sought so far away
　　I welcome at my door.

The airs of spring may never play
　　Among the ripening corn,
Nor freshness of the flowers of May
　　Blow through the autumn morn;

Yet shall the blue-eyed gentian look
　　Through fringéd lids to heaven,
And the pale aster in the brook
　　Shall see its image given; —

The woods shall wear their robes of praise,
  The south wind softly sigh,
And sweet, calm days in golden haze
  Melt down the amber sky.

Not less shall manly deed and word
  Rebuke an age of wrong;
The graven flowers that wreathe the sword
  Make not the blade less strong.

But smiting hands shall learn to heal, —
  To build as to destroy;
Nor less my heart for others feel
  That I the more enjoy.

All as God wills, who wisely heeds
  To give or to withhold,
And knoweth more of all my needs
  Than all my prayers have told!

Enough that blessings undeserved
  Have marked my erring track: —
That wheresoe'er my feet have swerved,
  His chastening turned me back; —

That more and more a Providence
  Of Love is understood,
Making the springs of time and sense
  Sweet with eternal good; —

That death seems but a covered way
  Which opens into light,
Wherein no blinded child can stray
  Beyond the Father's sight; —

That care and trial seem at last,
  Through Memory's sunset air,

Like mountain-ranges overpast,
In purple distance fair; —

That all the jarring notes of life
Seem blending in a psalm,
And all the angles of its strife
Slow rounding into calm.

And so the shadows fall apart,
And so the west winds play;
And all the windows of my heart
I open to the day.

240   *The Rock of Salvation.*

By FRANCIS S. KEY, born in Maryland in 1779; died in Washington 1843.
He is known as the author of "The Star-Spangled Banner."]

IF life's pleasures cheer thee,
  Give them not thy heart,
Lest the gifts ensnare thee
  From thy God to part:
His praises speak, His favor seek,
  Fix there thy hopes' foundation;
Love Him, and He shall ever be
  The Rock of thy salvation.

If sorrow e'er befall thee,
  Painful though it be,
Let not fear appall thee;
  To thy Saviour flee;
He, ever near, thy prayer will hear,
  And calm thy perturbation;
The waves of woe shall ne'er o'erflow
  The Rock of thy salvation.

Death shall never harm thee,
Shrink not from his blow,
For thy God shall arm thee,
And victory bestow:
For death shall bring to thee no sting,
The grave no desolation;
'Tis gain to die, with Jesus nigh,   •
The Rock of thy salvation.

241   *Subdued by the Cross.*

By Rev. JOHN NEWTON, born 1725; died 1807. He was the friend and
pastor of William Cowper. In this poem he records the history of his con-
version.]

IN evil long I took delight,
    Unawed by shame or fear,
Till a new object struck my sight,
And stopp'd my wild career.

I saw one hanging on a tree,
    In agonies and blood,
Who fix'd His languid eyes on me,
As near His cross I stood.

Sure, never to my latest breath
    Can I forget that look:
It seem'd to charge me with His death,
Though not a word He spoke.

My conscience felt and own'd the guilt,
    And plunged me in despair:
I saw my sins His blood had spilt,
And helped to nail Him there.

A second look He gave, which said,
    "I freely all forgive:

This blood is for thy ransom paid :
I die, that thou mayest live."
Thus, while His death my sin displays
In all its blackest hue,
Such is the mystery of grace,
It seals my pardon too.

242 *Glorying in the Cross.*

[Perhaps by JOHN BOWRING, LL. D., of England ; born 1792.]

IN the cross of Christ I glory,
Towering o'er the wrecks of time :
All the light of sacred story
Gathers round its head sublime.

When the woes of life o'ertake me,
Hopes deceive, and fears annoy,
Never shall the cross forsake me :
Lo ! it glows with peace and joy.

When the sun of bliss is beaming
Light and love upon my way,
From the cross the radiance streaming
Adds new lustre to the day.

Bane and blessing, pain and pleasure,
By the cross are sanctified :
Peace is there that knows no measure,
Joys that through all time abide.

In the cross of Christ I glory,
Towering o'er the wrecks of time :
All the light of sacred story
Gathers round its head sublime.

243   *Litany to the Holy Spirit.*

[By ROBERT HERRICK, 1648.]

IN the hour of my distress,
   When tempations me oppress,
And when I my sins confess,
      Sweet Spirit, comfort me.

When I lie within my bed,
Sick at heart and sick at head,
And with doubts disquieted,
      Sweet Spirit, comfort me.

When the house doth sigh and weep,
And the world is drowned in sleep
Yet mine eyes the watch do keep,   .
      Sweet Spirit, comfort me.

When the tempter me pursu'th
With the sins of all my youth,
And half damns me with untruth,
      Sweet Spirit, comfort me.

When the judgment is revealed,
And that opened which was sealed,
When to Thee I have appealed,
      Sweet Spirit, comfort me.

244   . *The Heart's Song.*

By ARTHUR CLEAVELAND COXE, D. D., Bishop of Western New York in
the Protestant Episcopal Church ; born in 1818, in New Jersey.]

IN the silent midnight watches,
   List thy bosom-door ;
 How it knocketh, knocketh, knocketh,
   Knocketh evermore !

Say not 'tis thy pulse's beating,
　'Tis thy heart of sin ;
'Tis thy Saviour stands entreating,
　" Rise and let me in."

Death comes down with equal footstep
　To the hall and hut ;
Think you death will stand a-knocking
　Where the door is shut ?
Jesus waiteth, waiteth, waiteth ;
　But thy door is fast ;
Grieved, at length away He turneth ;
　Death breaks in at last.

Then 'tis thine to stand entreating
　Christ to let thee in ;
At the door of heaven beating,
　Wailing for thy sin.
Nay, alas ! thou foolish virgin,
　Hast thou then forgot ?
Jesus waited long to know thee,
　But — He knows thee not.

245   *It is not Death to die.*

By GEORGE W. BETHUNE, D. D., LL. D., born in New York 1805 ; died
in Florence, Italy, 1862. A distinguished clergyman of the Reformed
Dutch Church.]

IT is not death to die,
　To leave this weary road,
And, midst the brotherhood on high,
　To be at home with God.

It is not death to close
　The eye long dimm'd by tears,

And wake in glorious repose
To spend eternal years.

It is not death to bear
The wrench that sets us free
From dungeon-chains, to breathe the air
Of boundless liberty.

It is not death to fling
Aside this sinful dust,
And rise on strong, exulting wing,
To live among the just.

Jesus, Thou Prince of Life,
Thy chosen cannot die!
Like Thee, they conquer in the strife,
To reign with Thee on high.

246 *Jesus, my Redeemer, lives.*

[By LOUISA HENRIETTA, Electress of Brandenburg, 1649, on the death of her son. Based on Job xix. 25-27 and 1 Cor. xv. A favorite hymn in Germany.]

JESUS, my Redeemer, lives,
  And His life I once shall see;
Bright the hope this promise gives,
  Where He is I soon shall be.
Shall I fear then? Can the Head
Rise and leave the members dead?

Ye who suffer, sigh, and moan,
  Fresh and glorious there shall reign;
Earthly here the seed is sown,
  Heavenly it shall rise again;
Natural here the death we die,
Spiritual our life on high.

Body, be thou of good cheer,
In thy Saviour's care rejoice,
Give not place to gloom and fear,
Dead thou yet shalt know His voice,
When the final trump is heard,
And the deaf cold grave is stirr'd.

Laugh to scorn then death and hell,
Laugh to scorn the gloomy grave;
Caught into the air to dwell
With the Lord who comes to save,
We shall trample on our foes,
Mortal weakness, fear, and woes.

Only see ye that your heart
Rise betimes from earthly lust;
Would you there with Him have part,
Here obey your Lord and trust.
Fix your hearts beyond the skies,
Whither ye yourselves would rise.

247 *Charity.*

[By Miss ADELAIDE A. PROCTOR.]

JUDGE´not; the workings of his brain
And of his heart thou canst not see;
What looks to thy dim eyes a stain,
In God's pure light may only be
A scar, brought from some well-won field,
Where thou wouldst only faint and yield.

The look, the air, that frets thy sight
May be a token that below
The soul has closed in deadly fight
With some infernal fiery foe,

Whose glance would scorch thy smiling grace,
And cast thee shuddering on thy face.
The fall thou darest to despise,
   May be the angel's slackened hand
Has suffered it, that he may rise
   .And take a firmer, surer stand;
Or, trusting less to earthly things,
May henceforth learn to use his wings.
And judge none lost; but wait and see,
   With hopeful pity, not disdain;
The depth of the abyss may be
   The measure of the height of pain
And love and glory that may raise
This soul to God in after days!

248 *Sin.*

[By "holy GEORGE HERBERT," born in Shropshire, England, 1593.]

LORD, with what care hast thou begirt us
   round!
   Parents first season us; then schoolmasters
Deliver us to laws; they send us bound
   To rules of reason, holy messengers;
Pulpits and Sundays, sorrow dogging sin,
   Afflictions sorted, anguish of all sizes,
Fine nets and stratagems to catch us in,
   Bibles laid open, millions of surprises;
Blessings beforehand, ties of gratefulness,
   The sound of glory ringing in our ears;
Without, our shame; within, our consciences;
   Angels and grace, eternal hopes and fears,—
Yet all these fences; and their whole array,
One cunning bosom-sin blows quite away!

249   *Bartimeus.*

[By Rev. JOHN NEWTON.]

MERCY, O thou Son of David!"
     Thus blind Bartimeus pray'd;
Others by Thy word are savéd,
     Now to me afford Thine aid:
Many for his crying chid him,
     But he call'd the louder still;
Till the gracious Saviour bid him,
     " Come, and ask me what you will."

Money was not what he wanted,
     Though by begging used to live;
But he ask'd and Jesus granted
     Alms, which none but He could give·
" Lord, remove this grievous blindness,
     Let my eyes behold the day:"·
Straight he saw, and, won by kindness,
     Follow'd Jesus in the way.

O methinks I hear him praising,
     Publishing to all around:
" Friends, is not my case amazing?
     What a Saviour I have found!
O that all the blind but knew Him,
     And would be advised by me!
Surely would they hasten to Him,
     He would cause them all to see."

250   *Morning at the Tomb.*

[By Rev. WILLIAM B. COLLYER.]

MORNING breaks upon the tomb:
     Jesus scatters all its gloom:

212

Day of triumph! through the skies
See the glorious Saviour rise!
Christian! dry your flowing tears;
Chase those unbelieving fears:
Look on His deserted grave;
Doubt no more His power to save.

Ye, who are of death afraid,
Triumph in the scattered shade;   •
Drive your anxious cares away:
See the place where Jesus lay!

Lo! the rising sun appears,
Shedding radiance o'er the spheres;
Lo! returning beams of light
Chase the terrors of the night.

251   *Night.*

[By Rev. THOMAS L. HARRIS.]

NIGHT prays with rosary of stars;
   The heavens and earth are still;
And prayer the Eden-world unbars
   To men of loving will.

We leave the city's shady streets,
   And seek the home of prayer;
And there the soul its Father meets;
   And angels lead us there.

Before the evening lamps were lit,
   The loving angels came,
With us to seek the Infinite,
   And own the Saviour's name.

Still, as we worship, they adore;
   In silent grace they stand;

And still our spirits they implore
To seek the Happy Land.

252   *Supplication.*

[By JEAN INGELOW.]

O GOD, O Kinsman loved, but not enough!
   O Man, with eyes majestic after death,
·Whose feet have toiled along our pathways
    rough,
Whose lips drawn human breath!

By that one likeness which is ours and Thine,
   By that one nature which doth hold us kin,
By that high heaven where sinless Thou dost
    shine
   To draw us sinners in,

By Thy last silence in the judgment-hall,
   By long foreknowledge of the deadly tree,
By darkness, by the wormwood and the gall,
   I pray Thee visit me.

Come, lest this heart should, cold and cast
    away,
   Die ere the Guest adored she entertain —
Lest eyes which never saw Thine earthly day
   Should miss Thy heavenly reign.

And deign, O watcher, with the sleepless brow,
   Pathetic in its yearning, — deign reply:
Is there, O is there aught that such as Thou
   Wouldst take from such as I?

253 ·   *" O Sacred Head."*

Written in Latin by the Catholic monk, St. BERNARD of Clairvaux, in 1153.
The first line of the original is " Salve caput cruentarum." Translated
into German by Paul Gerhardt, Lutheran, in 1656, his hymn beginning " O
Haupt voll Blutt und Wunder." Translated from Paul Gerhardt into English by Dr. James W. Alexander, an American Presbyterian, who died
1859, whose version begins " O Sacred Head, now wounded." Our version
is founded on that.]

O SACRED Head, now wounded ;
  With grief and shame weighed down !
O sacred brow surrounded
  With thorns, Thine only crown !
Once on a throne of glory,
  Adorn'd with light divine,
Now all despised and gory,
  I joy to call Thee mine.

On me, as Thou art dying,
  O turn Thy pitying eye !
To Thee for mercy crying,
  Before Thy cross I lie :
Lo ! here I fall, my Saviour !
  'Tis I deserve Thy place ;
Look on me with Thy favor,
  Vouchsafe to me Thy grace !

The joy can ne'er be spoken,
  Above all joys beside,
When, in Thy body broken,
  I thus with safety hide.
Lord of my life, desiring
  Thy glory, now I see ;
Beside Thy cross expiring,
  I'd breathe my soul to Thee.

What language can I borrow
  To thank Thee, dearest Friend,

For all Thy dying sorrow,
  Of all my woes the end ?
O can I leave Thee ever?
  Then do not Thou leave **me:**
Lord, let me never, never
  Outlive my love to Thee.

Be near me when I'm dying ;
  O show Thy cross to me ;
And to my succor flying,
  Come, Lord, and set me free :
These eyes, new faith receiving,
  From Thee shall never move :
For he who dies believing
  Dies safely in Thy love.

254   *The End.*

[By Rev. JOSIAH CONDER, an English Congregationalist ; born in 1790 ;
died in 1855.]

O THE hour when this material
  Shall have vanished as a cloud,
When amid the wide ethereal
  All th' invisible shall crowd, —
And the naked soul, surrounded
  With realities unknown,
Triumph in the view unbounded,
  Feel herself with God *alone!*

In that sudden, strange transition,
  By what new and finer sense
Shall she grasp the mighty vision,
  And receive the influence ?
Angels guard the new immortal,
  Through the wonder-teeming space,

To the everlasting portal,
  To the spirit's resting-place

Will she, then, with fond emotion,
  Aught of human love retain?
Or absorbed in pure devotion,
  Will no earthly trace remain?
Can the grave those ties dissever,
  With the very heart-strings twined?
Must she part, and part forever,
  With the friends she leaves behind?

No: the past she still remembers;
  Faith and hope surviving too,
Ever watch those sleeping embers,
  Which must rise and live anew:
For the widowed, lonely spirit,
  Waiting to be clothed afresh,
Longs perfection to inherit,
  And to triumph in the flesh.

Angels, let the ransomed stranger
  In your tender care be blessed,
Hoping, trusting, safe from danger,
  Till the trumpet end her rest, —
Till the trump which shakes creation
  Through the circling heavens shall roll,
Till the day of consummation,
  Till the bridal of the soul.

Can I trust a fellow-being?
  Can I trust an angel's care?
O Thou merciful All-seeing!
  Beam around my spirit there.

217

Jesus, blessed Mediator !
Thou the airy path hast trod :
Thou the Judge, the Consummator !
Shepherd of the fold of God.

255 *A Canticle of the Beloved.*

[We do not know the origin of this poem. It is more admired by many other persons than by the compilers of this volume, whose attention was called to it by the ardent praises of one of our most eloquent clergymen. It is manifestly modeled on the Song of Solomon, and may be preserved as a fair specimen of erotic devotional poetry.]

O THOU in whose presence my soul takes delight,
On whom in affliction I call, —
My comfort by day, and my song in the night,
My hope, my salvation, my all !
Where dost Thou at noontide resort with Thy sheep,
To feed on the pastures of love ?
For why in the valley of death should I weep,
Or alone in the wilderness rove ?
O, why should I wander an alien from Thee,
And cry in the desert for bread ?
My foes will rejoice when my sorrows they see,
And smile at the tears I have shed.
Ye daughters of Zion, declare, have you seen
The star that on Israel shone ?
Say, if in your tents my Beloved has been,
And where with His flocks He has gone ?
This is my Beloved, His form is divine,
His vestments shed odors around ;
The locks on His head are as grapes on the vine,
When autumn with plenty is crowned.
The roses of Sharon, the lilies that grow

In the vales on the banks of the streams,
On His cheeks in the beauty of excellence glow.
And His eyes are as quivers of beams.
His voice as the sound of the dulcimer sweet,
Is heard through the shadows of death ;
The cedars of Lebanon bow at His feet,
The air is perfumed with His breath.
His lips as a fountain of righteousness flow,
That waters the garden of grace ;
From which their salvation the Gentiles shall
know,
And bask in the smiles of His face.
Love sits in His eyelids, and scatters delight
Through all the bright mansions on high ;
Their faces the cherubim veil in His sight,
And tremble with fullness of joy.
He looks, and ten thousand of angels rejoice,
And myriads wait for His word;
He speaks, and eternity, filled with His voice,
Reëchoes the praise of the Lord.
His vestments of righteousness, who shall de-
scribe ?
Its purity words would defile :
The heavens from His presence fresh beauties
imbibe,
And earth is made rich by His smile.
Such is my Beloved, in excellence bright,
When pleased He looks down from above.
Like the morn when He breathes from the
chambers of light,
And comforts His people with love.

The portals of heaven at His bidding obey,
  And expand ere His banner appear;
Earth trembles beneath, till her mountains
    give way,
  And hell shakes her fetters with fear.
When He treads on the clouds, as the dust of
    His feet.
  And grasps the big storm in His hand,
What eye the fierce glance of His anger shall
    meet,
  Or who in His presence shall stand?

256   *Solace.*   C. M.
[By THOMAS MOORE, the Irish poet.]

O THOU who driest the mourner's tear.
    How dark this world would be,
If, when deceived and wounded here,
  We could not fly to Thee!

The friends who in our sunshine live,
  When winter comes, are flown;
And he who has but tears to give,
  Must weep those tears alone.

But Christ can heal that broken heart,
  Which, like the plants that throw
Their fragrance from the wounded part,
  Breathes sweetness out of woe.

O who could bear life's stormy doom,
  Did not Thy wing of love
Come brightly wafting through the gloom,
  Our peace-branch from above.

Then sorrow, touch'd by Thee, grows **bright,**
  With more than rapture's ray;

As darkness shows us worlds of light,
  We never saw by day.

258 **257**   *Good at Last.*

[By ALFRED TENNYSON, the poet laureate of England.]

O YET we trust that somehow good
  Will be the final goal of ill,
To pangs of nature, sins of will,
Defects of doubt, and taints of blood ;

That nothing walks with aimless feet ;
  That not one life shall be destroyed,
  Or cast as rubbish to the void,
When God hath made the pile complete ;

That not a worm is cloven in vain ;
  That not a moth with vain desire
  Is shriveled in a fruitless fire,
Or but subserves another's gain.

Behold, we know not anything ;
  I can but trust that good shall fall
  At last — far off — *at last,* to all,
And every winter change to spring.

So runs my dream : but what am I ?
  An infant crying in the night :
  An infant crying for the light :
And with no language but a cry.

258   *The Sleep.*

By ELIZABETH BARRETT BROWNING, born in England in 1809 ; died
                      1863.]

O F all the thoughts of God that are
  Borne inward into souls afar,
    Along the Psalmist's music deep,

Now tell me if that any is
For gift or grace surpassing this —
  " He giveth His beloved, sleep ? "

What would we give to our beloved?
The hero's heart to be unmoved,
  The poet's star-tuned harp to sweep,
The patriot's voice to teach and rouse,
The monarch's crown to light the brows? —
  He giveth His beloved, sleep.

What do we give to our beloved?
A little faith all undisproved,
  A little dust to overweep,
And bitter memories to make
The whole earth blasted for our sake:
  He giveth His beloved, sleep.

" Sleep soft, beloved ! " we sometimes say;
Who have no tune to charm away
  Sad dreams that through the eyelids creep:
But never doleful dream again
Shall break the happy slumber, when
  He giveth His beloved, sleep.

O earth, so full of dreary noises !
O men, with wailing in your voices !
  O delvéd gold, the wailers heap !
O strife, O curse, that o'er it fall !
God strikes a silence through you all,
  And giveth His beloved, sleep.

His dews drop mutely on the hill,
His cloud above it saileth still,
  Though on its slope men sow and reap :

More softly than the dew is shed,
Or cloud is floated overhead,
  He giveth His beloved, sleep.

Ay, men may wonder while they scan
A living, thinking, feeling man
  Confirmed in such a rest to keep;
But angels say, and through the word
I think their happy smile is heard, —
  " He giveth His beloved, sleep.".

For me, my heart that erst did go
Most like a tired child at a show,
  That sees through tears the mummers leap,
Would now its wearied vision close,
Would childlike on His love repose
  Who giveth His beloved, sleep.

And friends, dear friends, when it shall be
That this low breath is gone from me,
  And round my bier ye come to weep,
Let one most loving of you all,
Say, " Not a tear must o'er her fall !
  He giveth His beloved, sleep."

259 *Nearer Home.*

[By PHŒBE CARY. Written in New York in 1852. Many variations of this
poem have been published ; but the author desires the following to be considered hereafter her authorized version.]

ONE sweetly solemn thought
  Comes to me o'er and o'er ;
I'm nearer my home to-day
  Than I ever have been before :
Nearer my Father's house,
  Where the many mansions be ;

Nearer the great white throne.
　Nearer the crystal sea;
Nearer the bound of life,
　Where we lay our burdens down;
Nearer leaving the cross,
　Nearer gaining the crown:
But the waves of that silent sea
　Roll dark before my sight,
That brightly the other side
　Break on a shore of light.

O, if my mortal feet
　Have almost gained the brink,
If it be I am nearer home
　Even to-day than I think:
Father, perfect my trust,
　Let my spirit feel in death,
That her feet are firmly set　　　·
　On the Rock of a living faith!

260　　　　*Power and Love.*

[By Dr. Isaac Watts. Paraphrase of Psalm 147.]

PRAISE ye the Lord! 'tis good to raise　　·
　Your hearts and voices in His praise:
His nature and His works invite
To make this duty our delight.

He form'd the stars, those heavenly flames;
He counts their numbers, calls their names;
His wisdom's vast, and knows no bound, —
A deep where all our thoughts are drown'd.

Sing to the Lord! exalt Him high,
Who spreads the clouds along the sky;

There He prepares the fruitful rain
Nor lets the drops descend in vain.

He makes the grass the hills adorn ;
He clothes the smiling fields with corn ;
The beasts with food His hands supply,
And the young ravens when they cry.

What is the creature's skill or force ?
The sprightly man, or warlike horse,
The piercing wit, the active limb,
All are too mean delights for Him.

But saints are lovely in His sight ;
He views His children with delight :
He sees their hope, He knows their fear,
He looks, and loves His image there.

261   *Prayer.*

[By JAMES MONTGOMERY.]

PRAYER is the soul's sincere desire,
     Utter'd or unexpress'd ;
The motion of a hidden fire
     That trembles in the breast.

Prayer is the burden of a sigh, —
     The falling of a tear, —
The upward glancing of an eye,
     When none but God is near.

Prayer is the simplest form of speech
     That infant lips can try ;
Prayer, the sublimest strains that reach
     The Majesty on high.

Prayer is the Christian's vital breath,
     The Christian's native air ;

His watchword at the gates of death, —
He enters heaven with prayer.

Prayer is the contrite sinner's voice,
Returning from his ways;
While angels, in their songs, rejoice,
And cry, — Behold, he prays!

O Thou, by whom we come to God,
The Life, the Truth, the Way, —
The path of prayer Thyself hast trod : —
Lord, teach us how to pray!

262 *The Recall.*

[By Rev. W. B. Collyer, LL. D., an English Nonconformist; died in 1854.]

RETURN, O wanderer, return,
And seek thy Father's face;
Those new desires which in thee burn
Were kindled by His grace.

Return, O wanderer, return;
He hears thy humble sigh;
He sees thy soften'd spirit mourn,
When no one else is nigh.

Return, O wanderer, return;
Thy Saviour bids thee live:
Come to His cross, and, grateful, learn
How freely He'll forgive.

Return, O wanderer, return,
And wipe .the falling tear;
Thy Father calls, — no longer mourn;
'Tis love invites thee near.

Return, O wanderer, return ;
Regain thy long-sought rest :
The Saviour's melting mercies yearn
To clasp thee to His breast.

263   *New Year's Eve.*

[By ALFRED TENNYSON, poet laureate of England.]

RING out, wild bells, to the wild sky,
The flying cloud, the frosty light ;
The year is dying in the night ;
Ring out, wild bells, and let him die.

Ring out the old, ring in the new ;
Ring, happy bells, across the snow ;
The year is going, let him go ;
Ring out the false, ring in the true.

Ring out the grief that saps the mind,
For those that here we see no more ; •
Ring out the feud of rich and poor,
Ring in redress to all mankind.

Ring out a slowly dying cause,
And ancient forms of party strife ;
Ring in the nobler modes of life,
With sweeter manners, purer laws.

Ring out false pride in place and blood,
The civic slander and the spite ;
Ring in the love of truth and right,
Ring in the common love of good.

Ring out old shapes of foul disease,
Ring out the narrowing lust of gold ;
Ring out the thousand wars of old,
•Ring in the thousand years of peace.

Ring in the valiant man and free,
  The larger heart, the kindlier hand;
Ring out the darkness of the land,
Ring in the Christ that is to be.

264   *Salvation.*

[By Dr. ISAAC WATTS.]

SALVATION! O the joyful sound!
    What pleasure to our ears;
A sov'reign balm for every wound,
  A cordial for our fears.

Salvation! let the echo fly
  The spacious earth around,
While all the armies of the sky
  Conspire to raise the sound.

Salvation! O Thou bleeding Lamb!
  To Thee the praise belongs:
Salvation shall inspire our hearts,
  And dwell upon our tongues.

265   *To Sorrow.*

[By RICHARD MONCKTON MILNES.]

SISTER Sorrow! sit beside me,
    Or, if I must wander, guide me:
Let me take thy hand in mine;
Cold alike are mine and thine.

Think not, Sorrow, that I hate thee;
Think not I am frightened at thee;
Thou art come for some good end,
I will treat thee as a friend.

I will say that thou art bound
My unshielded soul to wound
By some force without thy will,
And art tender-minded still.

I will say thou givest scope
To the breath and light of hope;
That thy gentle tears have weight
Hardest hearts to penetrate;
That thy shadow brings together
Friends long lost in sunny weather
With an hundred offices
Beautiful and blest as these.

266 *Sudden Comfort.*

[By WILLIAM COWPER.]

SOMETIMES a light surprises
 The Christian while he sings:
It is the Lord who rises
 With healing in His wings:
When comforts are declining,
 He grants the soul again
A season of clear shining,
 To cheer it after rain.

In holy contemplation,
 We sweetly then pursue
The theme of God's salvation,
 And find it ever new.
Set free from present sorrow,
 We cheerfully can say,
Let the unknown to-morrow
 Bring with it what it may.

It can bring with it nothing,
　But He will bear us through :
Who gives the lilies clothing,
　Will clothe His people too ;
Beneath the spreading heavens,
　No creature but is fed ;
And He who feeds the ravens
　Will give His children bread.

Though vine nor fig-tree neither
　Their wonted fruit should bear,
Though all the fields should wither,
　Nor flocks nor herds be there :
Yet God the same abiding,
　His praise shall tune my voice;
For while in Him confiding,
　I cannot but rejoice.

267　　　*Sow beside all Waters.*

[By JAMES MONTGOMERY.]

SOW in the morn thy seed ;
　At eve hold not thy hand ;
To doubt and fear give thou no heed, —
　Broadcast it o'er the land.
Thou know'st not which shall thrive, —
　The late or early sown ;
Grace keeps the precious germ alive,
　When and wherever strown :
And duly shall appear,
　In verdure, beauty, strength,
The tender blade, the stalk, the ear,
　And the full corn at length.

Thou canst not toil in vain;
Cold, heat, and moist, and dry,
Shall foster and mature the grain
For garners in the sky.

268 *Bless the Lord.*

[By JAMES MONTGOMERY.]

STAND up, and bless the Lord,
Ye people of His choice;
Stand up, and bless the Lord your God,
With heart, and soul, and voice.

Though high above all praise,
Above all blessing high,
Who would not fear His holy name,
And laud, and magnify?

O for the living flame
From His own altar brought,
To touch our lips, our souls inspire,
And wing to heaven our thought!

God is our strength and song,
And His salvation ours;
Then be His love in Christ proclaimed
With all our ransomed powers.

Stand up, and bless the Lord;
The Lord your God adore;
Stand up, and bless His glorious name,
Henceforth, for evermore!

269 *Virtue.*

[By GEORGE HERBERT, born 1593.]

SWEET day! so cool, so calm, so bright;
The bridal of the earth and sky:

The dew shall weep thy fall to-night;
  For thou must die.
Sweet rose ! whose hue, angry and **brave,**
  Bids the rash gazer wipe his eye:
Thy root is ever in its grave :
  And thou must die.

Sweet spring! full of sweet days and **roses;**
  A box where sweets compacted lie;
My music shows you have your closes :
  And all must die.

Only a sweet and virtuous soul,
  Like seasoned timber, never gives;
But, though the whole world turn to **coal,**
  Then chiefly lives.

270   *Sitting at the Cross.*

This hymn has been assigned to many writers. In Denham's Collection it
is assigned to Robinson ; in Rider's " Lyra Anglicana " to Brydges ; while
Dr. Belcher positively declares Rev. Christopher Batty to have been the
author. Dr. Schaff says that this hymn appeared first in 1774, in Lady
Huntingdon's Hymn-book, which Rev. Walter Shirley revised, and that it
was originally written by Rev. James Allen, and revised by Shirley. It
has gone into the " Lyra Catholica " with the title " Sub Cruce Christi."
It is altered in every collection, and can be improved in very many more.]

SWEET the moments, rich in blessing,
  Which before the Cross I spend,
Life, and health, and peace possessing
  From the sinner's dying Friend.
Here I'll sit, forever viewing
  Mercy's streaming fount of blood ;
Precious drops, my soul bedewing,
  Plead and claim my peace with God.
Truly blesséd is this station ;
  Low before His Cross to lie,

While I see divine compassion
  Beaming from His earnest eye :
Here it is I find my heaven,
  While upon the Lamb I gaze.
Love I much ? I've much forgiven —
  I'm a miracle of grace.
Love and grief my heart dividing,
  With my tears His feet I bathe ;
Constant still in faith abiding,
  Life deriving from His death.
May I still enjoy this feeling,
  In all need to Jesus go ;
Prove His wounds each day more healing,
  And Himself more deeply know.

271   *The Judgment.*
[By HENRY HART MILMAN, D. D., Dean of St. Paul's, London.]

THE chariot ! the chariot ! its wheels roll
    in fire,
As the Lord cometh down in the pomp of His
    ire :
Lo, self-moving it drives on its pathway of
    cloud,
And the heavens with the burden of Godhead
    are bow'd.

The glory ! the glory ! around Him are pour'd
Mighty hosts of the angels that wait on the
        Lord ;
And the glorified saints and the martyrs are
    there,
And there all who the palm-wreaths of victory
    wear !

The trumpet ! the trumpet ! the dead have all
     heard :
Lo, the depths of the stone-cover'd charnel are
     stirr'd !
From the sea, from the earth, from the south,
     from the north,
All the vast generations of man are come
     forth !

The judgment ! the judgment ! the thrones
     are all set,
Where the Lamb and the white-vested elders
     are met !
There all flesh is at once in the sight of the
     Lord,
And the doom of eternity hangs on His word.

O mercy ! O mercy ! look down from above,
Great Creator, on us, Thy sad children, with
     love !
When beneath to their darkness the wicked
     are driven,
May our justified souls find a welcome in
     heaven !

272   *All's Well.*

THE day is ended. Ere I sink to sleep
     My weary spirit seeks repose in Thine;
Father, forgive my trespasses, and keep
     This little life of mine.

With loving-kindness curtain Thou my bed,
     And cool in rest my burning pilgrim feet;

Thy pardon be the pillow for my head —
   So shall my sleep be sweet.
At peace with all the world, dear Lord, and
      Thee,
   No fears my soul's unwavering faith can
      shake ;
All 's well, whichever side the grave for me
   The morning light may break !

273   *The God of Abraham.*

[" Blackwood's Magazine " pronounces this one of the noblest odes in the English language. It is by an early Methodist, the Rev. THOMAS OLIVERS.]

THE God of Abraham praise,
   Who reigns enthroned above :
Ancient of everlasting days,
      And God of love :
   Jehovah, great I Am !
      By earth and heaven confessed :
I bow and bless the sacred name,
      Forever blest.

The God of Abraham praise,
   At whose supreme command
From earth I rise, and seek the joys
      At His right hand :
   I all on earth forsake,
      Its wisdom, fame, and power ;
And Him my only portion make,
      My shield and tower.

He by himself hath sworn ;
   I on His oath depend ;
I shall on eagle's wings upborne
      To heaven ascend :

16   235

I shall behold His face,
I shall His power adore,
And sing the wonders of His grace
For evermore.

274   *The Glory of the Lord.*

[By STERNHOLD, written in 1540. Paraphrase of Psalm 18 : 9, 10. The learned Scaliger declared that he would rather be the author of the second stanza than of all that he had written.]

THE Lord descended from above,
And bowed the heavens most high,
And underneath His feet He cast
The darkness of the sky.

On cherubim and seraphim
Full royally He rode,
And on the wings of mighty winds
Came flying all abroad.

He sat serene upon the floods,   .
Their fury to restrain ;
. And He as sovereign Lord and King
For evermore shall reign.

275   *The Good Shepherd.*

[By JOSEPH ADDISON. Written in 1712. Paraphrase of Psalm 23.]

THE Lord my pasture shall prepare,
And feed me with a shepherd's care;
His presence shall my wants supply,
And guard me with a watchful eye:
My noonday walks He shall attend,
And all my midnight hours defend.

When in the sultry glebe I faint,
Or on the thirsty mountain pant,
To fertile vales and dewy meads

My weary, wand'ring steps He leads,
Where peaceful rivers, soft and slow,
Amid the verdant landscape flow.

Though in a bare and rugged way,
Through devious, lonely wilds I stray,
Thy bounty shall my pains beguile,
The barren wilderness shall smile,
With sudden greens and herbage crown'd,
And streams shall murmur all around.

Though in the paths of death I tread,
With gloomy horrors overspread,
My steadfast heart shall fear no ill,
For Thou, O Lord, art with me still :
Thy friendly crook shall give me aid,
And guide me through the dreadful shade.

276 *Dominion.*

[By Henry Kirke White, born in England, 1785 ; died in 1806.]

THE Lord our God is clothed with might,
　The winds obey His will ;
He speaks, and in His heavenly height
　The rolling sun stands still.

Rebel, ye waves, and o'er the land
　With threat'ning aspect roar ;
The Lord uplifts His awful hand,
　And chains you to the shore.

Ye winds of night, your force combine
　Without His high behest,
Ye shall not, in the mountain-pine,
　Disturb the sparrow's nest.

His voice sublime is heard afar ;
　In distant peals it dies ;
He yokes the whirlwind to His car,
　And sweeps the howling skies.

Ye sons of earth, in rev'rence bend ;
　Ye nations, wait His nod ;
And let unceasing praise ascend
　In honor of our God.

277　　　　　　*Thee, in all Things.*

[By " holy GEORGE HERBERT," born 1593. Rearranged and very slightly
altered.]

THE man that looks on glass
　On *it* may stay his eye,
Or, if he pleaseth, through it pass,
　And then the heaven espy.

All may of Thee partake :
　Nothing can be so mean
Which, when enacted for Thy sake,
　Will not grow bright and clean.

A servant with this clause,
　Makes drudgery divine :
Who sweeps a room, as for Thy laws,
　Makes that and the action fine.

Teach *me*, my God and King,
　In all things Thee to see ;
And what I do in anything,
　To do it as for Thee !

278 " *In the Midst of Life we are in Death.*"

This famous poem was written by a monk of St. Gall, named Notker, who lived in the beginning of the tenth century. It is preserved in the solemn magnificence of the English burial-service, in a form without poetic measure, but not without rhythm, beginning, " In the midst of life we are in death : of whom may we seek for succor but of Thee, O Lord ! " The hymn was suggested to the good monk by seeing the samphire-gatherers suspended on the sides of precipices ; and when he saw the bridge-builders at Martinsbruck exposing themselves in their perilous work, he prepared for his monastery this solemn hymn, which he and his brethren first chanted, and which in prose or verse has been said or sung for nearly a thousand years.]

THE pangs of death are near,
　Amid the joys of life ;
And when, in guilty fear,
　We end our dying strife,
To whom, most holy Lord,
　Shall we for succor flee ?
O Thou most mighty God !
　Our help is laid on Thee :
Lord Jesus ! by Thy bloody stains,
Save, save us from hell's bitter pains.

The bitter pains of hell
　Awaken our alarm ;
We merit only ill
　From Thine avenging arm ;
Most holy Lord our God,
　To whom but unto Thee,
Most merciful and good,
　Can we for refuge flee ?
Suffer us not to fall away
From Jesus, in our dying day.

Our dying day will come,
　And call our crimes to mind ;
And when, in sorrow dumb,
　No hope on earth we find,

239

To Thee, O Christ, we fly, —
　To Thine outflowing blood;
Look with Thy pitying eye,
　Spare us, most holy Lord:
Nor let us lose the joys that rise
From Thine atoning sacrifice.

279　　*Dedication of a Church.*

[By N. P. WILLIS, the American poet, born in Maine, 1807; died at Idlewild, 1867.]

THE perfect world by Adam trod,
　Was the first temple built by God:
His fiat laid the corner-stone,
And heaved its pillars, one by one.

He hung its starry roof on high —
The broad illimitable sky;
He spread its pavement, green and bright,
And curtained it with morning light.

The mountains in their places stood,
The sea, the sky, — and " all was good; "
And when its first pure praises rang,
The " morning stars together sang."

˙Lord ! 'tis not ours to make the sea
And earth and sky a house for Thee;
But in Thy sight our offering stands —
A humbler temple, " made with hands."

280   *Vexilla Regis.*

[From the Latin of Venantius Fortunatus of Italy, who was born 530, and died
609. He was the intimate friend of Queen Rhadegunda. This hymn is
sung in the Roman Catholic Church on Good Friday, when "the Host" is
carried to the altar. The version here given is, with some variations, that
of Rev J M. Neale, who considers this "one of the grandest in the treasury
of the Latin Church." The explanation of the last line of the third
stanza is, that in the Italic version, Ps. 96 : 10 reads, "Tell it among the
heathen that the Lord reigneth from the Tree." Justin Martyr accused
the Jews of corrupting the text, and Tertullian in several places quotes
the elder reading.]

THE royal banners forward go ;
   The cross shines forth in mystic glow ;
Where He in flesh, our flesh who made,
Our sentence bore, our ransom paid :

Where deep for us the spear was dyed,
Life's torrent rushing from His side,
To wash us in that precious flood
Where mingled water flowed, and blood.

Fulfilled is all that David told
In true prophetic song of old ;
Amidst the nations God, saith he,
Hath reigned and triumphed from the tree.

O tree of beauty, tree of light !
O tree with royal purple dight !
Elect on whose triumphal breast
Those holy limbs should find their rest ;

On whose dear arms, so widely flung,
The weight of this world's ransom hung :
The price of human kind to pay,
And spoil the spoiler of his prey.

281 *The Heavens declare His Glory.*

[This noble hymn has generally been attributed to Joseph Addison. It was
published in a number of the " Spectator" which Addison is known to
have written, but there he makes no claim to the authorship. The
"Athenæum" brings to light, from an old edition of his poems collected
in 1776, strong evidence that the hymn was written by Andrew Marvell.
There is no evidence that Addison was the author.]

THE spacious firmament on high,
    With all the blue ethereal sky,
And spangled heavens, a shining frame,
Their great Original proclaim :

The unwearied sun, from day to day,
Does his Creator's power display,
And publishes to every land
The work of an almighty hand.

Soon as the evening shades prevail,
The moon takes up the wondrous tale,
And nightly to the listening earth
Repeats the story of her birth :

While all the stars that round her burn,
And all the planets in their turn,
Confirm the tidings as they roll,
And spread the truth from pole to pole.

What though in solemn silence all
Move round this dark terrestrial ball ?
What though no real voice nor sound
Amid their radiant orbs be found ?

In reason's eye they all rejoice,
And utter forth a glorious voice,
For ever singing, as they shine,
" The hand that made us is divine."

282 *Resignation.*

[By HENRY WADSWORTH LONGFELLOW.]

THERE is no flock, however watched and
    tended,
But one dead lamb is there !
There is no fireside, howsoe'er defended,
    But has one vacant chair !
The air is full of farewells to the dying,
    And mournings for the dead ;
The heart of Rachel, for her children crying,
    Will not be comforted !
Let us be patient!   These severe afflictions
    Not from the ground arise,
But oftentimes celestial benedictions
    Assume this dark disguise.
We see but dimly through the mists and vapors ;
    Amid these earthly damps
What seem to us but sad, funereal tapers
    May be heaven's distant lamps.
There is no death ! What seems so is transition.
    This life of mortal breath
Is but a suburb of the life elysian,
    Whose portal we call Death.

283 *A City that hath Foundations.*

[By CHRISTINA G. ROSSETTI. Written in 1866.]

THEREFORE, O friend, I would not, if I
    might,
Rebuild my house of lies, wherein I joyed
One time to dwell : my soul shall walk in white,
    Cast down, but not destroyed.

Therefore in patience I possess my soul ;
　Yea, therefore as a flint I set my face,
To pluck down, to build up again the whole, —
　But in a distant place.
These thorns are sharp, yet I can tread on them ;
　This cup is loathsome, yet He makes it sweet ;
My face is steadfast toward Jerusalem,
　My heart remembers it.
I lift the hanging hands, the feeble knees, —
　I, precious more than　seven times molten
　　gold, —
Until the day when from His storehouses
　God shall bring new and old ;
Beauty for ashes, oil of joy for grief,
　Garment of praise for spirit of heaviness ;
Although to-day I fade as doth a leaf,
　I languish and grow less.
Although to-day He prunes my twigs with pain,
　Yet doth His blood nourish and warm my
　　root ;
To-morrow I shall put forth buds again,
　And clothe myself with fruit.
Although to-day I walk in tedious ways,
　To-day His staff is turned into a rod, —
Yet will I wait for Him the appointed days,
　And stay upon my God.

284　　*Fellowship of Suffering.*

[By **Theodore Tilton**, a native of New York.]

THY cruel crown of thorns !
　　But where, O Lord, is mine ?

Are there for me no scoffs and scorns,
  Since only such were Thine?
Or having named Thy name,
  Shall I no burden take?
And is there left no thorn, no shame,
  To suffer for Thy sake?

Unscourged of any whip,
  Unpierced of any sting, —
O Lord, how faint my fellowship
  With Thy sad suffering!
Yet Thy dread sacrifice
  So fills my soul with woe,
That all the fountains of mine eyes
  Well up and overflow.

The spear that pierced Thy side
  Gave wounds to more than Thee.
Within my soul, O Crucified,
  Thy cross is laid on me.

And as Thy rocky tomb
  Was in a garden fair,
Where round about stood flowers in bloom,
  To sweeten all the air, —

So in my heart of stone
  I sepulchre Thy death,
While thoughts of Thee, like roses blown,
  Bring sweetness in their breath.

Arise not, O my Dead!
  As one whom Mary sought,
And found an empty tomb instead,
  Her spices all for nought, —

O Lord, not so depart
  From my enshrining breast,
But lie anointed in a heart
  That by Thy death is blest.

Or if Thou shalt arise,
  Abandon not Thy grave,
But bear it with Thee to the skies, —
  A heart that Thou shalt save !

285   *Divine Order.*

[By Rev. HORATIUS BONAR, D. D., of Scotland. Published in 1856. Paraphrase of Rev. xxii. 20.]

'TIS first the true, and then the beautiful,
  Not first the beautiful, and then the true ;
First the wild moor, with rock and reed and pool,
  Then the gay garden, rich in scent and hue.

'Tis first the good, and then the beautiful,
  Not first the beautiful, and then the good :
First the rough seed, sown in the rougher soil,
  Then the flower-blossom, or the branching
    wood.

Not first the glad, and then the sorrowful,
  But first the sorrowful, and then the glad ;
Tears for a day, — for earth of tears is full, —
  Then we forget that we were ever sad.

Not first the bright, and after that the dark,
  But first the dark, and after that the bright ;
First the thick cloud, and then the rainbow's arc,
  First the dark grave, then resurrection light.

'Tis first the night, — stern night of storm and war,
  Long nights of heavy clouds and veiléd
    skies, —

Then the far sparkle of the morning-star,
That bids the saints awake, and dawn arise.

286 *Immortality.*

[By WASHINGTON ALLSTON, the great American painter, born in Charleston, S. C. ; died in 1843.]

TO think for aye ; to breathe immortal breath ;
   And know nor hope, nor fear, of ending
      death ;
To see the myriad worlds that round us roll
Wax old and perish, while the steadfast soul
Stands fresh and moveless in her sphere of
      thought ;
O God, omnipotent ! who in me wrought
This conscious world, whose ever-growing orb,
When the dead past shall all in time absorb,
Will be but as begun, — O, of Thine own,
Give of the holy light that veils Thy throne,
That darkness be not mine, to take my place,
Beyond the reach of light, a blot in space !
So may this wondrous life, from sin made free,
Reflect Thy love for aye, and to Thy glory be.

287 *Burial Psalm.*

[By Dr. ISAAC WATTS.]

UNVEIL thy bosom, faithful tomb ;
   Take this new treasure to thy trust ;
And give these sacred relics room
   To slumber in the silent dust.

Nor pain, nor grief, nor anxious fear
   Invade thy bounds : no mortal woes
Can reach the peaceful sleeper here,
   While angels watch the soft repose.

So Jesus slept; God's dying Son
  Pass'd through the grave, and blest the bed;
Rest here, blest saint, till from His throne
  The morning break, and pierce the shade.

Break from His throne, illustrious morn;
  Attend, O earth! His sovereign word;
Restore thy trust — a glorious form —
  Call'd to ascend and meet the Lord.

288   *Dying Christian to his Soul.*

[By ALEXANDER POPE.]

VITAL spark of heavenly flame!
  Quit, O quit this mortal frame!
Trembling, hoping, ling'ring, flying,
O the pain, the bliss of dying!
Cease, fond nature, cease thy strife,
And let me languish into life.

Hark! they whisper: angels say,
" Sister spirit, come away! "
What is this absorbs me quite —
Steals my senses. shuts my sight,
Drowns my spirit, draws my breath —
Tell me, my soul, can this be death?

The world recedes, it disappears!
Heaven opens on my eyes! my ears
  With sounds seraphic ring!
Lend, lend your wings! I mount, I fly!
O Grave, where is thy victory?
  O Death, where is thy sting?

289 *Morning Psalm.*

[By Bishop KEN, born in England 1637 ; died 1711.]

WAKE, and lift up thyself, my heart,
  And with the angels bear thy part,
Who all night long unwearied sing
High praise to the Eternal King.

I wake, I wake, ye heavenly choir,
May your devotion me inspire,
That I like you my age may spend,
Like you may on my God attend.

May I like you in God delight,
Have all day long my God in sight,
Perform like you my Maker's will,
O may I never more do ill.

Had I your wings, to heaven I'd fly,
But God shall that defect supply,
And my soul, wing'd with warm desire,
Shall all day long to heaven aspire.

290 *The House Above.*

[By CHARLES WESLEY.]

WE know, by faith we know,
  If this vile house of clay,
This tabernacle, sink below,
  In ruinous decay, —

We have a house above,
  Not made with mortal hands;
And firm as our Redeemer's love
  That heavenly fabric stands.

It stands securely high,
  Indissolubly sure :

Our glorious mansion in the sky
  Shall evermore endure.

Full of immortal hope,
  We urge the restless strife,
And hasten to be swallow'd up
  Of everlasting life.

Lord, let us put on Thee
  In perfect holiness,
And rise prepared Thy face to see,
  Thy bright, unclouded face.

Thy grace with glory crown,
  Who hast the earnest given;
And then triumphantly come down,
  And take us up to heaven.

291   *Harps on the Willow.*

[By Lord BYRON, born in England, 1788; died in Greece, 1824.]

WE sat down and wept by the waters
    Of Babel, and thought of the day
When our foe, in the hue of his slaughters,
    Made Salem's high places his prey;
And ye, O her desolate daughters!
    Were scatter'd all weeping away.

While sadly we gazed on the river
    Which rolled on in freedom below,
They demanded the song; but, O never
    That triumph the stranger shall know!
May this right hand be wither'd forever
    Ere it string our high harp for the foe.

On the willow that harp is suspended —
    O Salem! its sound should be free;

And the hour when thy glories were ended,
   But left me that token of thee :
And ne'er shall its soft tones be blended
   With the voice of the spoiler by me.

292   *Waiting is Serving.*

[By JOHN MILTON, author of " Paradise Lost," born 1608 ; died 1674.]

WHEN I consider how my light is spent,
   Ere half my days, in this dark world and
     wide,
And that one talent, which is death to hide,
Lodg'd with me useless, though my soul more
     bent
To serve therewith my Maker, and present
   My true account, lest he returning chide, —
   Doth God exact day-labor, light denied?
I fondly ask.   But Patience, to prevent
That murmur, soon replies, — God doth not
     need
   Either man's work, or His own gifts : who best
   Bear His mild yoke, they serve Him best : his
     state
Is kingly ; thousands at His bidding speed,
   And post o'er land and ocean without rest :
   They also serve who only stand and wait.

293   *Nativity of Christ.*

[By THOMAS CAMPBELL, of Scotland, author of " Pleasures of Hope," born
in 1777 ; died 1844.]

WHEN Jordan hush'd his waters still,
   And silence slept on Zion's hill, —

When Bethleh'm's shepherds through the
   night
Watch'd o'er their flocks by starry light, —
Hark! from the midnight hills around,
A voice of more than mortal sound
In distant hallelujahs stole,
Wild murm'ring o'er the raptured soul.

Then swift to every startled eye
New streams of glory light the sky;
Heaven bursts her azure gates to pour
Her spirits on the midnight hour.

On wheels of light, on wings of flame,
The glorious hosts of Zion came;
High heaven with songs of triumph rang,
While thus they struck their harps and sang:

"O Zion, lift thy raptured eye,
The long-expected hour is nigh,
The joys of nature rise again,
The Prince of Salem comes to reign.

"He comes, to cheer the trembling heart,
Bids Satan and his hosts depart:
Again the day-star gilds the gloom,
Again the bowers of Eden bloom."

294   *The Sweetness of Faith.*

[By Rev. Aug. M. Toplady, of England.]

WHEN languor and disease invade
   This trembling house of clay,
'Tis sweet to look beyond its walls,
   And long to fly away;

Sweet to look inward, and attend
　The whispers of His love;
Sweet to look upward to the place
　Where Jesus pleads above;

Sweet to look back, and see my name
　In life's fair book set down;
Sweet to look forward, and behold
　Eternal joys my own:

Sweet on His faithfulness to rest,
　Whose love can never end;
Sweet on His covenant of grace
　For all things to depend.

If such the sweetness of the stream,
　What must the fountain be
Where saints and angels draw their bliss
　Directly, Lord, from Thee?

295　　　　*Star of Bethlehem.*
[By HENRY KIRKE WHITE, of England, born in 1785; died in 1806.]

WHEN, marshaled on the nightly plain,
　The glittering host bestud the sky,
One star alone of all the train
　Can fix the sinner's wandering eye.

Hark, hark; to God the chorus breaks,
　From every host, from every gem;
But one alone the Saviour speaks,
　It is the Star of Bethlehem.

Once on the raging seas I rode,
　The storm was loud, the night was dark;
The ocean yawned, and rudely blowed
　The wind that tossed my foundering bark.

Deep horror then my vitals froze,
　　Death-struck, I ceased the tide to stem ;
When suddenly a star arose —
　　It was the Star of Bethlehem.

It was my guide, my light, my all,
　　It bade my dark forebodings cease ;
And, through the storm and danger's thrall,
　　It led me to the port of peace.

Now, safely moored — my perils o'er —
　　I'll sing, first in night's diadem,
Forever, and for evermore,
　　The Star — the Star of Bethlehem.

296   *How much I owe.*

[By Rev. ROBERT MURRAY McCHEYNE, a saintly young clergyman of the
Free Church of Scotland, born 1813 ; died 1843.]

WHEN this passing world is done,
　　When has sunk yon glaring sun,
When we stand with Christ in glory,
Looking o'er life's finished story,
Then, Lord, shall I fully know —
Not till then — how much I owe.

When I stand before the throne,
Dressed in beauty not my own,
When I see Thee as Thou art,
Love Thee with unsinning heart,
Then, Lord, shall I fully know —
Not till then — how much I owe.

When the praise of heaven I hear,
Loud as thunder to the ear,
Loud as many waters' noise,

Sweet as harp's melodious voice,
Then, Lord, shall I fully know —
Not till then — how much I owe.

297 *Sailor's Hymn.*

[By REGINALD HEBER, Bishop of Calcutta.]

WHEN through the torn sail the wild tempest is streaming,
When o'er the dark wave the red lightning is
gleaming,
Nor hope lends a ray the poor seaman to cherish,
We fly to our Maker — "Save, Lord! or we
perish!"

O Jesus! once toss'd on the breast of the billow,
Arous'd by the shriek of despair from Thy pillow,
High now in Thy glory the mariner cherish,
Who cries in his anguish, "Save, Lord! or we
perish!"

And O, when the storm of wild passion is raging,
When sin in our hearts its fierce warfare is wag-
ing,
Arise in Thy strength Thy redeemed to cherish,
Rebuke the destroyer — "Save, Lord! or we
perish!"

298 *Watch.*

WHILST the careless world is sleeping,
Blest the servants who are keeping
Watch, according to His Word,
For the coming of their Lord.

At His table He will place them,
With His royal banquet grace them,
  Banquet that shall never cloy;
  Bread of life and wine of joy.

Heard ye not your Master's warning?
He will come before the morning,
  Unexpected, undescried;
  Watch ye for Him open-eyed.

Teach us so to watch, Lord Jesus;
From the sleep of sin release us:
  Swift to hear Thee let us be,
  Meet to enter in with Thee.

299   *Haste not, rest not.*

From the German of GOETHE, who was born 1749; died 1832. This poem
written in 1768.]

WITHOUT haste! without rest!
  Bind the motto to thy breast;
Bear it with thee as a spell;
Storm or sunshine, guard it well!
Heed not flowers that round thee bloom:
Bear it onward to the tomb!

Haste not! let no thoughtless deed
Mar for aye the spirit's speed!
Ponder well and know the right,
Onward, then, with all thy might!
Haste not, years can ne'er atone
For one reckless action done.

Rest not! life is sweeping by,
Go and dare before you die:
Something mighty and sublime

Leave behind to conquer time!
Glorious 'tis to live for aye,
When these forms have passed away.

Haste not! rest not! calmly wait;
Meekly bear the storms of fate!
Duty be thy polar guide, —
Do the right, whate'er betide!
Haste not! rest not! conflicts past,
God shall crown thy work at last.

300   *Without Thy Presence.*

[By FRANCIS QUARLES, of England, born 1592.]

WITHOUT Thy presence earth gives no re-
        fection;
Without Thy presence sea affords no treasure;
Without Thy presence air's a rank infection;
    Without Thy presence heaven itself no pleas-
        ure:
If not possess'd, if not enjoy'd in Thee,
What's earth or sea or air or heaven to me?

The highest honors that the world can boast
    Are subjects far too low for my desire;
The brightest beams of glory are (at most)
    But dying sparkles of Thy living fire.
The loudest flames that earth can kindle, be
But nightly glow-worms, if compared to Thee.

Without Thy presence wealth is bags of cares;
    Wisdom but folly; joy disquiet — sadness:
Friendship is treason, and delights are snares,
    Pleasures but pain, and mirth but pleasing
        madness.

Without Thee, Lord, things be not what they be,
Nor have they being when compared with Thee.
In having all things, and not Thee, what have I?
   Not having Thee, what have my labors got?
Let me enjoy but Thee, what further crave I?
   And having Thee alone, what have I not?
I wish nor sea nor land; nor would I be
Possessed of heaven, heaven unpossessed of
    Thee.

INDEX TO FIRST LINES.

INDEX TO FIRST LINES.

INDEX TO FIRST LINES.

INDEX TO FIRST LINES.

INDEX TO FIRST LINES.

INDEX TO FIRST LINES.

www.ingramcontent.com/pod-product-compliance
Lightning Source LLC
Chambersburg PA
CBHW030351270326
41926CB00009B/1055